NEW TRENDS IN READING INSTRUCTION

by Shelley Umans

TEACHERS COLLEGE PRESS
Teachers College · Columbia
University · New York

© 1963 by Teachers College, Columbia University
Library of Congress Catalog Number: 63–11708

Third Printing, 1970

Printed in the United States of America

Preface

This book was written in an effort to share with others some of the newer approaches to reading instruction. Schools throughout the country are experimenting with less traditional methods of organization, and it has been my experience that administrators and teachers alike need guidance in trying these new approaches.

The New York City public-school system, being the largest in the world, serves students who are representative of almost every type of community in the country. Students of small suburban communities, average-sized industrial cities, mobile communities, in-migrant communities, and rural communities all live within its boundaries. Therefore, as consultant in charge of reading for the junior high schools of New York City, I have had the opportunity to work with the widest range of teachers and students.

At no time in this book do I intend to minimize the problem of introducing new programs; nor, on the other hand, do I concede that change presents too many difficulties to be practical. Scientific advances and new learning theories have stimulated new instructional approaches. Added content and more demanding standards have made it more necessary than ever for teachers and students alike to be provided with the skills needed in order to achieve. A new look at reading instruction is timely.

Writing a book means more than gathering materials. It is, in a way, a culmination of one's professional experiences. I would like, therefore, to acknowledge and thank, not only those people who have contributed to the content of the book, but also those who have shared with me their knowledge and experience in the field of reading. I wish to thank the members of the Junior High School Reading Teams, whose lesson plans I have included here; Mr. William Schorkopf, who assisted me in evaluating much of the content; Mrs. Grace Goodell, who has been my co-worker in many projects; my husband, whose suggestions and advice have been of much value; Dr. Hamden L. Forkner, who has counseled me in each step in the preparation of this manuscript; Dr. Ruth Strang, who—as my teacher—was a guiding influence; and Dr. Joseph Loretan, associate superintendent in charge of junior high schools in New York City, who has given me direction and encouragement in initiating new approaches to the teaching of reading.

SHELLEY UMANS

Contents

1 Introduction   **1**

A Look at Reading Instruction Today   1

Reconsiderations   2

Definition of Terms   3

Selecting a Reading Program   3

2 Reading in the Subject Disciplines   **5**

Planning a Schoolwide Program   6

*Establishing the need for intensive work in
reading 7 Planning grade and departmental
conferences 8 Setting up the program with
the classroom teacher 10 The role of the
school librarian in different library plans 11*

Patterns of Instructional Organization   13

*The Sewanaka experiment 14 The New York
City project 14*

Instructional Practices and Materials   19

*English language arts 19 Social studies 27
Mathematics 33 Science 38 Industrial Arts
42*

Evaluating the Program   46

*Standardized tests 46 English language arts,
46 Social studies 48 Mathematics 48 Sci-*

vii

ence 49   *Informal (teacher-made) tests* 49
English language arts 51   *Social studies* 52
Mathematics 54   *Science* 55

Suggested Reading   57

3   Flexible Grouping in Reading Instruction   59

The Teaching Team in Flexible Grouping   60

Advantages for the student 62   *Advantages for the teacher* 62

Setting Up the Teaching Team   62

The team leader 62   *Participating teachers* 63   *Observing teachers* 63   *Student teachers* 66   *Teacher assistants* 67   *Mobility within the team* 67

Selecting the Team Pattern   68

Pattern 1: Participating teachers given other assignments 68   *Pattern 2: Team leader in training* 68   *Pattern 3: Participating teachers attend* 69

Selection of Groups   70
Scheduling Classes   71

In secondary schools 71   *In elementary schools* 72

Encouraging the Students to Participate   73
Planning   73
Large-Group Reading Lessons   76
Materials of Instruction   77

Chalkboards 77   *Overhead projectors* 77   *Charts* 84   *Flannelboards* 84   *Tape recorders* 84   *Duplicated materials* 85   *Disc recordings* 85

Team Orientation for Teachers   85

Workshops 85   *Resource persons* 86   *In-service program for teachers* 86

Adapting to the School Plant   86

Getting the most out of available space 88
Desk room 88   *dark shades* 88   *electrical
outlets* 88   *ventilation* 88   *acoustics* 89

Films, Filmstrips, and Slides in Flexible
Grouping   89

Films—16mm 90   *Filmstrips* 91

Television in Flexible Grouping   92

Experiments in television teaching 92   *The
Cortland television experiment* 98   *The Dade
County experiment* 98   *The Hagerstown experiment* 98

Language Laboratories in Flexible Grouping   99

Self-Selection (Individualized Reading) for
Flexible Grouping   100

Evaluation of the Program   101

Standardized tests 102   *Informal (teacher-
made) tests* 102   *Student and faculty reactions* 102

Suggested Reading   104

**4   Programed Materials in Reading
Instruction**   **105**

The Constructed Response (Linear Programing)   106

Branching (Intrinsic Programing)   112

Teaching Machines Versus Programed Textbooks   114

Programing Versus Conventional Methods   114

*How does the programed textbook differ from
a workbook?* 115   *How does the programed
textbook differ from a textbook?* 115   *How
does the programed textbook differ from a
classroom lesson?* 116   *How does the programed textbook differ from a film or telecast?* 117   *How does the programed textbook
differ from a test?* 117

Other Uses of Programing   117

Programing Reading   118

Steps in Programing   121

Programing and the Curriculum   130

Introducing Programed Materials   131

Evaluating Programed Materials   133

The Future of Programing   135

Suggested Reading   136

5   Community Resources   137

The Intellectual Resource Pool Used Outside School   138

    Seminar 1: Analyzing newspaper articles 139
    Seminar 2: Analyzing poems 139

The Intellectual Resource Pool Used in School   140

Public Education Groups (School Volunteers)   140

Reading Counseling and Teaching Centers   143

Suggested Reading   145

NEW TRENDS
IN READING
INSTRUCTION

1 Introduction

The primary goal of a reading program is to help each student develop the ability to think in a reading situation. The school's organization for reading, the quality of instruction, and the instructional materials employed will, in great part, determine how effectively a student reaches the point at which he reads well.

Reading is a staple in the instructional program—a base on which all learning is built. A student with poor reading ability and low achievement in his academic subjects finds it difficult to obtain recognition, even in the subjects which require little or no reading. If he is placed in a section with slow readers, his potential talents in other areas tend to be overlooked. This is unfortunate but too often a fact of life.

A Look at Reading Instruction Today

See Yellow Book P. 160

Perhaps, because of its importance, educators have been loath to "meddle with" reading instruction. Organization for reading instruction has changed little in the past few decades. Grouping procedures are pretty much the same, with flexibility allowed only within the rigid structure of a conventional classroom. As one of the trilogy of "R's," reading is still thought of as a tool subject, one that stands apart from content. Yet each subject area requires reading skills of a special nature, skills that are an integral part of the content. As the content becomes increasingly difficult, so the ability to read becomes more demanding. Reading materials have been geared to the "normal reader" with little provision for those students who need more time and more practice to learn. Individualizing instruction, more often than not, means that a teacher divides her time among the students, using very much the same materials, rather than differentiating instruction with multi-level materials. Furthermore, the teaching of reading, for the most part, is a school-oriented subject with the school personnel taking the full responsibility for instruction. Little has been done to involve members of the community in helping to extend reading experiences.

Reconsiderations

The static quality of reading organization is now being questioned. School systems are attempting new organizational patterns. In the move to individual instruction, programed learning materials (teaching machines) are being developed which allow a student to move at his own pace and learn and reinforce only those skills that require emphasis. Administrators are beginning to schedule students to meet in groups of varying sizes. The number 30 is no longer "magic." Some lessons lend themselves to large-group audiences, whereas others are best presented to individuals or small groups. Subject-area teachers are becoming aware of the necessity to help their students read content material effectively. Although basic reading skills are necessarily taught in the early grades, specific skills are being identified and introduced as soon as the content becomes specialized. Reading experiences are being extended and school systems are reaching out beyond the textbook. They are finding that the community can offer a wealth of primary sources. Members of the community are now being invited to share their knowledge with students, to supplement and enrich the reading program.

It is still too soon to evaluate the effectiveness of these programs. Very often, just the novelty and excitement of a new approach can stimulate students to greater achievement. But, too often, when the excitement wears off, learning recedes. However, in each of these approaches there may be some qualities that will make an important contribution to reading instruction, and only with trial and error will we discover what they are.

In considering any of these approaches, please note that suggested school organizations, like sample lesson plans, are merely structures from which to deviate. Each school administrator, as well as each teacher, will look at an organization plan or a lesson plan and say, "How can I adapt (*not* adopt) this to best meet the needs of my students?"

Definition of Terms

No matter what approach is used, a school-wide reading program must provide for students with varying reading abilities. A *developmental program* for students who are able readers should be a continuous sequential program of reading instruction, and should reinforce and extend those desirable reading skills and appreciations acquired in previous years, and develop new skills of appreciation as they are needed to comprehend and enjoy advanced and complex forms of written communication.

Those students who have reading disabilities and are one or two years behind what might be expected of them require a *corrective reading program*. Some of these students may be reading "on grade level" but, because of their ability, should be reading several years "above grade level."

On the other hand, a *remedial reading program* would be necessary for those students who have major problems in addition to a reading disability—problems which the classroom teacher and reading specialist are not equipped to handle. Such students should be referred to a special reading clinic where they can receive help from psychiatrists, psychologists, or social workers, as well as from a reading therapist. Not every one will use the above terms in the same way, but they are so designated for the purpose of reference.

In each school system, titles may differ, but responsibilities tend to remain the same. A reading consultant in one system may be called a reading coordinator or a reading specialist in another system. A superintendent in one system may have the same responsibilities as a director of instruction in another. Therefore, may I suggest that, despite the designation, the position be identified by its function.

Selecting a Reading Program

This book is directed toward those people who are interested in and responsible for reading improvement in our schools: members of the school boards, school superintendents, school principals, reading consultants, librarians, classroom teachers, parents, and publishers of educational materials. In looking at new programs, each of the above, regardless of his particular role, might ask these questions: Will this program improve reading instruction? Is this program suitable to the needs of the students? Is the professional staff prepared to implement the program? Are there adequate instructional materials? How will we know whether or not the program is effective? Is the climate of the school such that the teachers and the students will try new approaches?

Innovation is always disturbing, disrupting, and suspect. Even with the very best of intent and preparation, it is difficult to effect change. The purpose of this book is to help educators to introduce newer approaches to reading organizations, always, however, with the reservation that little is new, that what works for some may not work for others, that a generation may pass before a program can truly be evaluated, and that the subject of our program—the learner—possesses more variables than have ever been identified.

2   Reading in the Subject Disciplines

Although a sound foundation in basic skills and abilities in reading is necessary to the teaching of reading in literature, science, social studies, mathematics, etc., a sound reading program, whether on the secondary or elementary level, should make provision for developing the particular skills and understandings inherent in each of the various subject fields. It is generally recognized that somewhere about the fourth grade reading material becomes more highly specialized in subject content. Before that level is reached, the emphasis is on reading competencies of a general nature. Lee[1] supports this view, saying that, before a child in grade four, five, or six can hope for success in the content subjects, he should have a basic reading ability of at least the fourth-grade level. He should be able to identify most words he meets in his school work correctly and quickly. He should be able to relate the meanings of these words to the particular material he is reading. He should be able to identify the purpose for which he is reading, read at an appropriate speed and be able to comprehend the selection. Finally, he should be able to evaluate and react to what he has read. These skills are the necessary reading competencies of a *general* nature.

As pupils add subject textbooks to their basal reading materials, they are faced with a large number of new words; this is unlike the situation posed by the basal reader, where the practice is to repeat a limited number of new words many times. Reference materials in subject areas introduce many more facts than do basal readers. Each subject area has

[1] Doris May Lee, *The Importance of Reading for Achieving in Grades Four, Five, and Six,* Bureau of Publications, Teachers College, Columbia University, New York, 1933, p. 60.

a vocabulary peculiar to it, and each area also has familiar terms which take on new meanings.

Studies have shown that the ability to read adequately in one subject area does not in itself insure the ability to read adequately in another subject area. The skills necessary for the reading of social studies are quite different from the skills necessary for reading mathematics, or the skills needed for proficiency in reading literature. Therefore, instructional provision must be made for the special abilities called for in the reading required for each subject area. Improving a student's ability to read specific content material will improve his general reading ability as well.

Until recently the elementary school was held entirely responsible for the development of whatever reading ability the student acquired. This approach was impractical and unrealistic. The degrees of reading competency vary with each educational level, and reading skills should be taught not only in the elementary schools but in the secondary schools as well. Thus, it has become the responsibility of the English teacher in the secondary schools to continue the teaching of the reading skills.

One of the dangers of this is that the English teacher often limits the skills he teaches to only those necessary for reading literature—a limitation imposed by the subject area. Who, then, will teach the skill of reading a mathematics problem, of classifying facts in the science laboratory, of drawing inferences from the social studies text, of following directions in the industrial arts shop? Reading presents these special problems in the subject areas where there are *specific reading skills* required to read and understand the content of the curriculum. Because of this, each subject teacher must teach reading as well as his own subject.

However, since the subject teacher does not normally receive training in this phase of his subject, it becomes the obligation of the school principal and the reading consultant (if the school has one) to construct in-service programs for the subject teachers. In this way, the reading skills will, in time, become an integral part of every subject course.

Planning a Schoolwide Program

To set up these in-service programs, a reading consultant can, with the assistance of skilled and interested teachers, plan general faculty conferences and staff, grade, and department conferences relative to reading. If there is no reading consultant in the school, an assistant to the principal might take on the responsibility for this program. In the teaching of reading in the special subject areas, all members of the professional staff are involved, and it is most important that each feel himself a part of an integrated program. Once the decision to do in-service work in reading has been made, the program might look like the one described in detail below. Any program will certainly include many of the elements described.

Establishing the need for intensive work in reading

One of the most difficult tasks is to help subject-matter teachers see the necessity of teaching skills directly related to the reading of the particular subject. Somehow, the feeling persists that reading is always taught "elsewhere" and "at another time."

A general faculty meeting should be called to discuss with the entire professional staff the need for a reading skills program and the fact that all the subject disciplines must share the responsibility for developing their respective programs.

At this general faculty meeting, research studies to support the need for teaching reading of subject matter, might be brought to the attention of the staff. For example, a study by Maney[2] reports that a generalized reading ability does not exist and that content and purpose dictate the nature of the skills to be employed in reading a particular selection. To read material in the subject areas, a student must set a purpose for reading so that he knows which facts to select and which to reject as unimportant to his purpose. Students must learn how to vary their reading speeds to achieve the depths of understanding which match the purposes for which they read. Artley[3] reports that various studies clearly show that a particular field of knowledge makes demands for reading interpretation which do not duplicate those in other fields. The factors in each field which determine the special basic abilities are: (1) its aim, (2) the inherent nature of the material, (3) the symbolism it uses, (4) its characteristic methods of instruction, and (5) the type of problem being solved.

These studies point to the need for the content teacher to understand that each subject has its own characteristic reading skills and that a knowledge of them is necessary in order to master the content of the curriculum.

The annual testing program should be discussed at the meeting with

[2] Ethel S. Maney, "Literature and Critical Reading in Science," *Journal of Experimental Education,* 27:57–64 (September 1958).

[3] A. Sterl Artley, "Critical Reading in Content Areas," *Elementary English,* 36:122–130 (February 1959).

the faculty. It might be pointed out, for example, that if an achievement battery such as the *New Metropolitan* or the *Stanford Achievement* is administered, the scores given in each of the curriculum areas will merely give the achievement of pupils as tested by a given set of questions and not the reason for that achievement. Whether incorrect answers were due to a lack of knowledge or an inability to read the questions, cannot be determined by these tests. Instruments such as the *Sequential Test of Educational Progress* (*STEP*) and the *Iowa Test of Educational Development* (*ITED*) can measure, to a limited extent, the student's ability to read and comprehend questions as well as his knowledge of content.

The purpose of a general faculty meeting is not only to present the need of a developmental reading program in the subject areas through a discussion of research findings and an interpretation of test results; it also gives the members of the staff an opportunity to ask questions and present specific problems they meet in their classrooms. Through this type of conference a teacher may discover that teaching reading is a necessary adjunct to successful mastery of content.

Planning grade and departmental conferences

Once there is agreement as to the need for special efforts in reading, the next step might be to call grade meetings (or department meetings on the secondary level) to plan an appropriate reading program. If there is a reading consultant, he will act in an advisory capacity at each of these meetings. He is the teacher-supervisor to the classroom teacher, a resource person for new methods and instructional materials in all aspects of reading. He is familiar with techniques of teaching reading and of the existing research in reading, the latest texts published, and the professional journals and monographs.

The first meeting or series of conferences should usually be devoted to an *analysis of what is to be taught*. This calls for the group to: (1) study the curriculum and determine which sections are appropriate for the teaching of reading skills; (2) identify those reading skills required for the successful reading of content; (3) determine in which sequence the skills should be taught; (4) survey the required texts, the supplementary materials, and the trade books that will be available for use.

A reading consultant can help the teacher analyze the test results by making an item analysis to ascertain on which specific questions the students made errors. This can be done by returning the answer sheets to the students and allowing each student to report on a paper (identified only by a number) other than his own. The teacher asks the students to raise their hands if an item corresponding to the number called has been answered incorrectly. The teacher records on his copy of the test the number of hands raised for a particular item and, in a matter of moments, he determines which items were missed by the greatest number of pupils. The teacher then identifies the specific skill that is needed to answer each question correctly. With this type of information, the test becomes more meaningful to both the teacher and the student.

The teacher may then wish to distribute the original tests so that the students can see which questions presented difficulties. Did they have difficulty in following the instructions for answering the questions? Could they find the main idea or central thought of the passage? Did they know how to infer what was asked if it was not specifically stated in the question? Was the vocabulary unfamiliar or the concepts too remote? On the basis of discovering specific difficulties, the teacher may proceed to plan the reading improvement program. Those questions missed by the greatest number of students would indicate the skills which need immediate reteaching. Depending upon the number of items, such an analysis can be carried out in about ten or twenty minutes, for a one-period test.

The next departmental or grade conference might include a demonstration lesson given by a competent teacher. If a reading consultant is available, he can assist the subject teacher in planning the lesson. This lesson should be planned in detail, stating the specific skill to be taught, the reason for choosing the particular skill, and its place in the curriculum. The teacher attending the demonstration lesson should receive a copy of the lesson plan prior to the lesson presentation.

The demonstration lesson would be a short one, as the reading portion of a subject-area lesson should not consume an entire period. A discussion period following the demonstration enables teachers to ask questions about the lesson. New teachers, especially, need help in learning how to adapt basic lessons to classes of diverse reading abilities. Sometimes the same lesson can be used for several classes with different reading abilities by merely varying the vocabulary and changing the exercises. In this way, fewer preparations are necessary and the teacher has additional time to plan lessons.

The demonstration lesson serves as a model, and the teachers should be encouraged to adapt it to fit the needs, levels, and interest of their students. The inexperienced teacher may present the demonstration lesson much as it was originally given, whereas the more experienced teacher may change it entirely.

Every demonstration lesson should be followed up by a discussion and *evaluation of the lesson.* Some may find the demonstration too difficult for their group, or that, because of a wide range of reading ability in the class, provision for more differentiated instruction is necessary. Others may find that the lesson covered much of what the student already knew and that facets of the lesson need not be taught in their classrooms. This type of analysis, would then be followed by a second demonstration lesson given in another reading skill, perhaps by the same teacher who gave the first demonstration. Other teachers should be encouraged to give demonstration lessons as they become more experienced and secure in their teaching of reading lessons.

The cycle could then continue throughout the school year: planning, conference, demonstration, application to individual needs, evaluation. However, during the school year, changes in conference procedures may suggest themselves. For example, as the teachers become more experienced in the analysis of demonstration lessons, they may discontinue demonstrations with students and may use the conference period solely for discussion of suggestions and evaluation of teaching approaches.

The reading consultant, in addition to conducting whole staff conferences and departmental conferences, works individually with administrators, librarians, classroom teachers and assisting members of the faculty of local universities. In the teaching of reading in the special subject areas, all members of the professional staff are involved, and it is most important that each feel himself part of an integrated program.

Setting up the program with the classroom teacher

Since each discipline has its own method of presenting information by means of the printed word, a content subject teacher should be able to help his students to read a mathematics book, a history book, an atlas, a science text, or an industrial arts work sheet. To plan a reading-skills program in a particular subject area, the teacher, perhaps with the help of a reading consultant, should first locate the textbooks suited for a particular class. Since, in any one classroom, there is usually a range of reading ability, no one text could be read by all students. For example, in a single classroom there may be three groups, with as much as a year's reading difference from group to group. The content demands, however, are the same for all the students. The problem, then, is to find textbooks on three different reading levels covering the content requirements. Some book publishers recognize this need and publish companion series in which the same content is presented on three different reading levels. For example, the same fifth grade class studying the western movement in social studies would have three textbooks all discussing the Oregon Trail, each written on a different reading level. Each student would then choose the book he was capable of reading and would learn as much about the Oregon Trail as his classmates. After each student has been assigned a book he can read, the teacher is then ready to introduce the specific skills pertinent to the reading of the subject.

The reading consultant can help the subject teacher to develop these lessons. This will be discussed in detail in the section of this chapter on instructional materials, on pages 19 through 45.

The classroom teacher should evaluate the quality of new books and make suggestions to book publishers recommending improvements in future editions. A new book should be ordered in small quantities so that the teacher can distribute them to a test group of students before mass orders are placed.

A reading consultant can help the content area teacher create bulletin board displays. Some excellent suggestions are offered by the Fearon Book Company in San Francisco, publishers of a series of paperback booklets on the many uses of bulletin boards. Some of their publications are *E-2 Bulletin Boards, Baited Bulletin Boards* and, the most recent, *Bulletin Boards That Teach.* This last include specific suggestions in the curriculum areas of arithmetic, health, industrial arts, music, and science.

Professional publications should be ordered for the school library. A classroom teacher's personal budget and lack of knowledge of specific publications often limit him in building a professional library. A reading consultant can take the responsibility of ordering books for teachers and seeing to it that they are circulated. Some of the more recent publications in the teaching of reading in the content areas are mentioned in the suggested readings at the end of the chapter.

The role of the school librarian in different library plans

The ultimate aim of reading instruction is the application of its learnings to both functional and recreational reading. An early New England settler gave these rules for improving one's reading ability:

Read
Read some more,
Read things you yourself enjoy
Read and talk about it
Read very carefully some things
Read on the run most things
Don't think about reading, but—
READ

Librarians, more than anyone else, would agree with the advice of this early settler. The school librarian is in a key position to help to develop coordinated extensive reading programs. In the teaching of content reading, pupils should be encouraged to extend their reading within a subject. For example, books such as *Great Men of Mathematics* by E. T. Bull, *Money Go 'Round* by J. J. Flaherty, *From Z to Infinity* by Constance Reid, and *Excursions in Mathematics* by Ernest R. Breslich will greatly enrich a student's understanding of the field of mathematics.

Llewellen's *Earth Satellite,* Ludovici's *The World of the Microscope,* Freeman's *Fun With Astronomy,* and Irving's *Hurricanes and Twisters* are examples of helpful supplemental reading materials in science. In social studies, books on contemporary problems should be made available to students while they are studying world history. A file of current articles and publications, properly catalogued, will make it possible for students to become aware of some of the recent thinking on the subject.

The librarian should be prepared to guide students in selecting books on their particular reading levels that will inform them in the subject being studied. In order to do this, a librarian must work closely with the classroom teacher to become familiar with curriculum requirements, the unit the class is presently studying, and the individual interests of students. A good librarian will learn to know her students and on occasion recommend specific books that she thinks they will enjoy. A personal approach of this nature is very effective in motivating children to read.

One method of organizing a school library system is to decentralize and maintain the library room primarily for reference materials such as encyclopedias and journals. Large numbers of books are then circulated on a "loan basis" to subject classrooms. When a fifth grade class is studying the western movement, all books on that topic would be sent to that particular classroom and become part of a classroom library. As soon as the unit is completed, these books would be transferred to another class about to study the same subject. Under this procedure children are surrounded by the books directly applicable to the subject under immediate study. Too often children lose their desire to read a particular book if there is a long waiting period between library visits.

Another plan now being used in a number of school libraries is the "open schedule." Under this plan, students need not wait for regularly assigned library periods but may go to the library whenever they need reading materials pertinent to their classwork. Aside from consulting the librarian if they need help in finding appropriate books or in locating specific information, the students function independently. The open schedule, while having many of the advantages of the decentralized classroom library, has the additional advantage of making available a full complement of books for the students' use.

A competent librarian observes students as they read and carry out research assignments in the library, and reports to the classroom teacher when certain students appear to need help in specific reading skills. For example, a student who copies whole. paragraphs from an encyclopedia is lacking in the skill of note taking and outlining. The librarian, noting that a student takes a long time to read a book, may decide to inform the teacher, as the student may need practice in improving his rate of reading. Students who are constantly asking the librarian for pronunciations and meanings of words might need help in word recognition skills and in the use of the dictionary.

There are times when the librarian may do direct teaching. If a student uses the encyclopedia to the exclusion of other resources, the librarian may help the student to learn the value of a variety of reference materials. A student who has difficulty locating information in a book might need instruction in how to use the index, chapter headings, and marginal notes. At times, a whole class can be given a lesson by the librarian in the use of a new set of reference books or in the location of articles in publications. Many adult students as well as school-age students shy away from resource publications for information because they are unfamiliar with them. The librarian, the reading consultant, and the teacher should form a resource team for the selection, the use of, and the distribution of books.

Patterns of Instructional Organization

The school principal should be interested in organizations which make imaginative and creative instruction possible. For example, an elementary school principal may wish to follow the Pittsburgh Plan, whereby fourth, fifth, and sixth grade teachers are subject specialists and each teacher teaches his own subject to all the students assigned to those grades. These teacher specialists are also responsible for teaching the reading skills of their own particular subject. In other school systems, elementary pupils remain in their classrooms while teachers are rotated during part of the school day; subject specialists travel from class to class. Each subject specialist teaches reading skills as part of the content of the course of study.

The Sewanaka experiment

An experiment is now in progress in Sewanaka Central High School in Floral Park, New York, in which social studies content is taught through the reading skills. Unlike other programs, this one does not include time set aside for reading instruction per se. A reading skill is introduced in the social studies classroom, and the selection used to present this skill relates to the content of the social studies curriculum. Practice exercises are on related content materials. Instruction is given by the regular social studies teacher, with the reading consultant assisting in planning and preparation of materials.

Because many of the teachers participating in the Sewanaka experiment do not have training in the teaching of reading skills, they need the assistance of a reading consultant. Curriculum guides have been developed that include the skills to be taught, suggested lesson plans, the special vocabulary of social studies, and comprehension selections. All of the materials are on three levels of difficulty to provide for the range of reading abilities of the students in the experiment. Through this experiment the school hopes to discover whether this approach to social studies increases efficiency in learning to read and, as a result, whether the student gains a more thorough understanding of the subject.

The New York City project

New York City is working on a plan to improve the reaching of reading in content areas in the junior high schools by means of a demonstration-teaching approach. Teams of reading consultants work with teachers who have less than five years experience in the teaching of reading in English, social studies, science, mathematics, and industrial arts. The reading consultants present demonstration lessons in regular classroom situations at the invitation of the teacher.

The reading consultants were selected because of their special training, experience in teaching reading, and ability to understand problems of classroom teachers. The reading supervisor (the present author) provided special preparatory workshops and conferences to prepare the consultants for their role in this reading improvement program.

In one school year, each reading team is assigned to work successively in six junior high schools whose principals have requested this assistance. Every reading team consultant works with a group of participating teachers in the various content areas. The reading team spends the first week of each six-week training period in an orientation program which includes group conferences, a study of the school plan, a study of available instructional materials, and the diagnostic procedures used in a school and a study of the school population. For the next five weeks the following plan is followed with each participating teacher:

1. A demonstration reading lesson is given by the reading consultant in one of the participating teacher's regularly scheduled content classes.

2. A conference between the consultant and the participating teacher follows the demonstration lesson. This conference includes a discussion of the lesson observed, an explanation of the skill taught and its place in the curriculum, and the planning of a follow-up lesson that the participating teacher would present in the presence of the reading consultant.

3. The jointly planned follow-up lesson is then presented by the participating teacher. A conference follows this lesson so that the reading consultant and the classroom teacher can discuss the effectiveness of the lesson and plan the next lesson that is to be given by the reading consultant. The cycle then starts again with demonstration, conference, classroom-teacher-participation lesson, and conference.

4. Panel workshops are planned and parents are invited to participate in weekly meetings. Sometimes these take the form of reading consultants, subject teachers and parents working together in the preparation of materials. At other times, parents and teachers take turns in discussing the reading program as each one sees it.

Four features make this a significant project. First, the special reading skills required for reading in various subject areas are taught to whole classes by members of the team acting as demonstration teachers. Although the teachers of these classes and other faculty members involved in the activities benefit from this on-the-job demonstration project, the chief focus is the student. Second, the approach is developmental, using the regular junior high school curriculum and the text books and instructional materials available in the school, and drawing upon the teacher's plans as they reflect the needs of the students. Third, the plan uses the team of specialists to involve whole school staffs for six-week periods of intensive review of their instructional approaches. The individual students thus receive reading instruction throughout the whole school day as each of their teachers complements and supplements the others' efforts. Fourth, parents are invited to discuss the reading problems of their children individually and in groups.

To show the details of this particular program, a plan of operation for the six weeks is outlined in Exhibit I.

The approach outlined in Exhibit I is just one example of how assistance can be brought to the classroom teacher. Its special strength is that it enables the teacher to observe a "live lesson" with his own students. A research team from Teachers College, Columbia University, conducted a recent study of this project and found that this demonstration approach produced significant improvements in teaching practices.

Dr. Conant commented on this demonstration teacher training approach in his recent publication, *Slums and Suburbs*. He stated:

. . . Very important from my point of view, is a team project designed for in-service teacher training. The purpose is to improve the teaching of reading in all subject areas, not just English. Seven teams of three expert teachers each go into the schools—one team to a school—for six weeks and conduct demonstration classes for the teachers. My staff was very much impressed with what they saw.[4]

Another approach to organizing a school for the teaching of reading in the content subjects is to provide for ability groups and to teach the specific skills needed at each ability level. For example, the student who is having difficulty with mathematics is placed in a section where he can get assistance both with the subject matter and with the reading skills of mathematics. Another student needing help in subject matter may not need reading instruction and would be placed in another group. Some of these same students may excel in science and be placed in the top group where they will learn both subject matter and reading skills needed to understand science materials. The plan takes into account the varying reading levels a pupil may achieve in various subjects.

[4] James Bryant Conant, *Slums and Suburbs*, McGraw-Hill, New York, 1961, p. 59.

Exhibit I

Plan of Operation

Organizational and Planning Period

Participants:
Principal; assistant in charge of reading; reading consultant; head of English department (optional); assistants in charge of other subject areas (optional).

Purposes and Activities:
1. Review and interpret for the supervisors the purposes and operation of the project.
2. Plan with supervisors the operation of the project by:
    a. choosing participating staff personnel
    b. choosing participating classes
    c. planning schedule of conferences and activities for the introductory week.
    d. planning observation schedule
    e. planning procedure for introducing the project to the participating students.
3. Arrange organizational detail by:
    a. working out programs of team members
    b. providing team members with schedules and materials

First Week of Team Operation
(Orientation period)

Participants:
Principal; assistant in charge of reading; reading consultant; team members; participating teachers.

Purposes and Activities:
To introduce the staff to the project, its goals and operation:
1. Establish a workshop in the "how" and "why" of teaching reading in all subject areas:
    a. large-group conferences
    b. small-group conferences
    c. individual conferences
    d. setting tone and relationships
2. Become acquainted with the school, teachers, and pupils.
3. Study the assigned classes:
    a. note interests, aptitudes, and problems

Exhibit I (*Continued*)

b. note reading strengths and needs
c. note existing materials and methods
4. Complete initial planning.

Second Through Fifth Weeks

(Demonstration, conference, and teacher-participation period)
Participants:
Principal; assistant in charge of reading; reading consultant; team members; participating teachers; observing teachers; pupils.

Purposes and Activities:
To improve the teaching of reading and thereby improve reading ability.
1. Demonstrations:
    a. identify reading needs
    b. teach reading skills in all curriculum areas
    c. select and utilize varied and suitable reading materials
    d. integrate and vitalize corrective reading instruction
    e. develop techniques pertinent to classroom management and class control
2. Conferences, group and individual:
    a. interpret demonstration purposes and techniques
    b. implement reading source materials
    c. focus on the "why" and "how" of planning
    d. build basic concepts and understandings in reading
3. Teacher participation:
    a. apply teaching techniques demonstrated by team member
    b. extend teaching techniques to other reading activities

Sixth Week
(Concluding procedures)

Participants:
Principal; assistant in charge of reading; reading consultant; team members; participating teachers; observing teachers.

Purposes and Activities:
To bring operation to a profitable and satisfactory conclusion:
1. Elicit and summarize values of project
2. Plan follow-up activities
3. Select and duplicate effective and valuable materials to be left in the school

In the junior high schools and senior high schools departmentalization can facilitate ability grouping if one does not adhere to block programing. It becomes more difficult in the elementary school, unless subject specialists are part of the organization.

Instructional Practices and Materials

Since a general reading ability is not a substitute for the specific abilities needed in each subject area, the first step in teaching reading of content material is to identify the skills that make a reader efficient. The reading consultant, together with the subject teacher, after identifying the specific skills, should plan reading lessons. The following section is devoted to a description of some of the skills in each of five subject areas: English language arts, social studies, mathematics, science, and industrial arts. Sample lessons are given to demonstrate the integration of reading lessons and content lessons.

The English language arts

The English language arts include a great variety of reading skills. There are the basic reading skills such as the ability to recognize new words, find the main thoughts of paragraphs and articles, and identify and understand the relationship between main idea and supporting detail. There are also special vocabulary and comprehension difficulties connected with the teaching of literature. In addition to the wide range of words involved, there are nuances and impressions created by the style of language, by certain combinations of words and phrases, and by the association of ideas. Pupils must be taught how to interpret and appreciate creative writing, how to identify an author's mood, his interest and purpose in writing. In poetry, the student must learn how to read between the lines to understand an impression or an emotion the poet wishes to convey.

To be an efficient reader in the English language arts, one should be able to:

1. understand word meanings by using context clues, syllabication, structural analysis, and phonics.
2. understand and appreciate literature by
    a. getting the general significance through identifying the stated or inferred main ideas in paragraphs, chapters, books, poetry,

scenes from plays and other literary selections.
b. seeing that details, inferred or stated, support, illustrate, and add color and life.
c. recognizing the author's purpose in writing, and evaluating the reliability and relevance of the context.
d. adjusting reading speed to the purpose.
3. read printed material effectively by:
a. locating and using source material: the parts of a book, the card catalogue file, the *Reader's Guide to Periodical Literature,* newspapers, etc.
b. organizing ideas in proper sequence and logical order.
c. outlining ideas that they may be effectively retained and presented in the form desired.

Exhibits II, III, and IV outline the types of reading lessons that might be used in the English language arts.

Exhibit II

Direct Reading Lesson Outline

Skill:
Comprehension. This is a whole-story lesson. It is designed to suggest a way of teaching a whole story within one period. Pupils may have been assigned a first reading of the story as homework, but the development of the reading skills within the story are done in the class period.

Approach (Motivation):
Use pictures or realia to create interest in the material or topic involved in the story. If the story has a locale in another country, point up the relationship between the geographic features and the people—use a map. If another racial group is involved, show pictures in order to relate story characters to the setting. Use any illustrative material that will make pupils *want to know* more about the people involved.

Direct teaching techniques:
1. *Vocabulary development:*
   Select, from the story, words that need to be taught. These must be presented within the context of the story. Try to have pupils get the meanings themselves via contextual or analytical word skills. Use dictionary, if that is appropriate. Write words and meanings on chart or board.
2. *Whole story reading:*
   Have pupils read the whole story *silently* and *purposefully*. Assign one big question as the aim for reading. If the teacher feels the whole story is too much of a bite for the class, this step may be done by pages, with a question assigned for *purposeful* reading. After giving an adequate amount of time for reading, briefly question pupils on the assigned material.

Exhibit II (*Continued*)

3. *Oral reading:*
The teacher asks specific questions, refers to specific paragraphs, asks pupils to find the answers, *study these answers,* and *prepare them to be read orally.* Examples: Find the sentence that tells us whether or not Carlos enjoyed the fair—study it, and prepare to read it orally; or, find the sentence that tells us how beautiful the streets of Costa Rica are—study it, and prepare to read it orally. *Make sure that any oral reading is purposeful and prepared.*
4. *Written work:*
Carefully word three or four questions that would embrace varying types of thinking on the part of pupils, such as:
   a. question for the searching out of details
   b. question involving reasoning
   c. question involving inference
   d. question involving a personal opinion resulting from some action in the story

Summary:
A summary in a directed reading lesson may consist of a review of the steps necessary to read and understand a complete story—steps such as:
1. Understanding new vocabulary.
2. Setting a purpose for reading.
3. Reading to answer specific questions.
4. Reading with understanding, so as to be able to react.

Follow-up:
Such a lesson may or may not be completed in one period. The written work may be done in a subsequent lesson. The pupils' work should be criticized constructively by the teacher and evaluated by the class. Draw attention to the fact that the thought question may have many and varying answers, and all may be correct.

Exhibit III

Lesson Outline for Topics and Subtopics

Skill:
Developing the ability to condense sentences into shorter expressions that retain the main thought.
Supplementary skill:
Understanding sentences. Finding the main idea of paragraphs.

Approach (Motivation):
1. Develop recognition of the purpose of today's reading skill in the following manner.
   a. Demonstrate the way a newspaper headline suggests the contents of the article it introduces.
   b. Show that the headline is a condensed version of the main idea sentence of the first or "lead" paragraph of the article.
   c. Evoke the conclusion that the main thought of the sentence is retained in the headline, even though the sentence is condensed.
2. Elicit from pupils the following uses of condensing sentences in their school subjects:
   a. Note taking in preparation for giving a report (research).
   b. Note taking while listening to others give oral reports.

Direct teaching techniques:
1. Present a paragraph to be read silently. Have pupils find the main idea sentence of the paragraph and the detail sentences that support it.
2. Determine the "core" of the main idea sentence by having pupils find the answers to the following types of questions:
   a. *Who* or *what* did something in this sentence?
   or
   Who or *what* had something done to *him* or *it*?
   b. *What* did some *person* or *thing do* in this sentence?
   or
   What was done to some *person* or *thing*?

Exhibit III (*Continued*)

3. Write the "core" or condensed version of the main idea sentence (topic sentence) on the board and direct pupils' attention to the following:
   a. The condensed expression (topic) retains the thought of the sentence.
   b. The first word of the condensed version (topic) begins with a capital letter.
   c. No mark of punctuation is used after the condensed expression (topic).
4. Using the techniques described in steps 2 and 3 above, change each supporting sentence of the paragraph (step 1) into a condensed expression that retains the thought (subtopic).

Summary:
Review the purpose of today's reading skill and stress its importance and use in various school experiences.

Follow-up:
1. Reinforce the learnings of today's lesson by performing the following activities:
   a. Have pupils bring to class copies of newspaper articles to prove the validity of the following statements: (1) Headlines highlight important events. (2) Headlines indicate the content of the articles they introduce. (3) Newspaper articles may sometimes be summarized from their headlines.
   b. Prepare a section of the bulletin board to display the pupils' work on the newspaper article brought to class.
   c. Have pupils take notes on specific paragraphs read aloud to them. Check the condensed expressions (topics and subtopics) written by the pupils during the reading.
   d. Continue using sentences from paragraphs, selected from various subject area textbooks, as purposeful practice of this skill.

Exhibit IV

Lesson Outline in Finding the Main Idea

Skill:
Finding the main idea of a paragraph.
Supplementary skill; locating supporting details.

Approach (Motivation):
1. Present several unrelated sentences arranged in paragraph form:

We had a wonderful time at the party. I cried all the way home from the funeral. It was an exciting football game. Yesterday we saw a movie. My brother lost his way on the subway.
2. Have pupils read the "paragraph" silently, to find out what it is about.
3. Elicit from pupils the conclusion that the "paragraph" does not tell about one idea, since no one sentence supports another. In most paragraphs they read, every sentence relates to one idea.

Direct teaching techniques:
1. Ask specific questions requiring detailed answers about one topic in the subject area.
   a. What sort of time did you have when you and your friends went to a very good party?
   b. What sort of food did you eat, and how much?
   c. What sort of music and dancing occurred?
   d. How was the room decorated?
   e. What type of clothes were the boys and girls wearing?
2. Place pupils' answers on the board in paragraph form.
3. Write three titles for the paragraph on the board, such as:

Plenty of Good Food

Wonderful Party

Rock 'n Roll Music

Have pupils choose the best one. The one chosen is best because it applies to the entire paragraph.

Exhibit IV (*Continued*)

4. Have pupils locate the sentence in the paragraph that helped them choose the title, and call one pupil to the board to underline that sentence, such as:

<u>We had a wonderful time at the party.</u>

Elicit from pupils the conclusion that this sentence gave the main idea.

5. Compare the paragraph on the board to a locked door. How do we unlock the door to take something valuable stored behind it? (We use a key.) How do we unlock the paragraph to take out its meaning? (We find a sentence.) Elicit from pupils the term "key sentence," and remind them that most well-written paragraphs contain key sentences.

6. Ask pupils how we know that the sentence we have chosen is the key sentence. Evoke the answer that there are *details* in the *other sentences* which prove, or support, it. Have pupils point out these details at the board.

   a. good food
   b. rock 'n roll music
   c. pretty decorations
   d. party clothes

7. Have pupils read silently one or two paragraphs of selected material to locate the key sentence of each paragraph plus the details in other sentences that prove which sentences are the key sentences.

Summary:

1. Ask class to tell the way to find the main idea of a paragraph and elicit the following guide:

   To find the main idea,
   a. read the whole paragraph,
   b. look for the key sentence, and
   c. find detail in the paragraph to prove or support the key sentence.

2. In what way does this skill help us in this subject? In other subjects?

Follow-up:

1. Have pupils copy into their notebooks steps they used in finding the main idea.

2. Continue using several paragraphs of selected material, following the procedure developed in step 7 above.

Social studies

Social studies requires the learner to identify central issues in the factual material used. He must be familiar with the special vocabulary and be able to adjust his rate of reading to the kind of material and the purpose for which it is being read. He should be able to recognize underlying assumptions to evaluate evidence and appraise authority. In social studies, more than in any other subject, he must learn to think and read critically.

In order to be an effective reader of the social studies, the student should be able to:

1. Recognize and understand its vocabulary and note exact meanings.
2. Understand social studies concepts by:
   a. Finding main ideas in sentence, paragraphs, etc.,
   b. Noting how details support and illustrate main ideas,
   c. Organizing ideas and outlining for understanding, review, and presentation,
   d. Relating ideas and drawing inferences,
   e. Understanding time and space relationships.
3. Read and study effectively by:
   a. Adjusting rate and depth of comprehension to the purpose,
   b. Using survey methods such as SQ3R (Survey Question, Read, Recite, Review),
   c. Understanding visual and graphic materials such as globes, charts, graphs, and diagrams,
   d. Using library skills to locate and use information for research,
   e. Taking useful notes.

Exhibits V and VI give examples of how reading skill lessons can be integrated with social studies content.

Exhibit V

Lesson Outline in Map Reading

Skill:
Using the legend or key.
Supplementary skill:
Special meanings of words in social studies context.

Approach (Motivation):
1. Write the following on the chalkboard:

Legend	Symbol	Key
English	Math	Shop
Social Studies	Social Studies	Social Studies

2. Ask students to define "legend," "symbol," and "key" as they would be used in each subject area.
3. In today's lesson we will learn the meanings of these words as they are used in social studies.
4. Place these words singly on the board asking this question. "When you drive along a highway and see this color in a light or on a sign, what word flashes to mind?" (Write the responses given under the colors.)

red	yellow	green
Stop	Caution	Go

5. "What word flashes to mind when you see these signs?" Show road symbols:

Drive in this direction.	Road curves.	Approaching a railroad crossing.

6. Elicit from students:
   a. These are two types of codes.
   b. A color code and symbol code are typical codes.
   c. They are used in place of words.
7. Question: "Why are codes such as these used on highways in place of words?" Develop the understanding that the use of these is economical in terms of space and quickness of mental response.
8. Just as these traffic codes help us to understand the safety signs along the road so today we are going to learn to read some codes which will help us to understand the maps in our textbook. The map codes are called legends or keys.

Direct teaching techniques:
1. Most maps have a legend.
2. A legend, as used in social studies, is sometimes called a key.

Exhibit V (*Continued*)

3. A legend or key is generally found in the margin of the map near one of the corners.
4. A legend or key contains information that will help us to use and understand the map.
5. A legend generally has:
   a. coded information which can be found on the map,
   b. a scale of miles to determine distances,
   c. sometimes, the title of the map.
6. The information coded on the legend is related to the title of the map and the map's contents. This code helps us to find the information we are seeking on the map.
7. There are different types of codes used in different map legends.
8. The types used in the legends on the maps in a book may be colors, numbers, symbols such as lines and dots, plus a combination of colors and symbols.
9. Using a map,
   a. have pupils locate the legend, introducing the term legend;
   b. note where it is placed in relation to the map.
10. Direct pupils attention to the first item of the legend, the title.
   a. have pupils identify the important words in the title: "political," "physical."
   b. review meanings of these words.
   c. bring out fact that these words give us a clue as to what information will be decoded.
11. Direct pupils to the legend code.
   a. What are the physical aspects that will be indicated on the map?
   b. What type of code will be used to indicate these? Answer, "color."
12. Direct pupils in a study of the code to discover the information that is given next to each of the seven color variations.
13. Direct pupils in an application of the code, using, for example, a map of New York State:
   a. Find Long Island on the map. Note the color used. Check the color against the color in the legend. Note the information given next to this color. Answer this question: "How high above sea level are parts of Long Island?"
   b. Find Lake Ontario on the map. Locate the darker blue area in the lake. Check this color against the color key. Answer this question: "How many fathoms deep is this part of the lake?" (Special assignment: a report on "How deep is a *fathom*?")
   c. Question: "How high above sea level are the Catskill Mountains? Direct pupils in following these steps: find the key words in the question, locate the Catskill Mountains on the map, note the color,

Exhibit V *(Continued)*

check it against the key, note the information given, answer the question.

    d. Follow the steps in using the color code to answer this question: "We are taking a trip from New York City to Albany by the most direct route. What is the range of the height of the land over which we will travel?"

14. Return to the legend of the map. Direct pupils to find the following information given in this legend:
    a. symbols for state capitols and railroads;
    b. variation in type to show sizes in town and cities;
    c. the scale of miles.
15. Leaf through the book, note and discuss:
    a. why some of the maps have no legend;
    b. some have only one symbol to be identified and used.
16. Direct pupils to the subtitle, "Key to Population of Cities and Towns."
    a. Discuss the meaning of the word "key" as used here.
    b. Note information given in this key.
    c. Note variation in type.
17. Follow steps outlined to answer the first of the questions listed below the map which involve the use of the legend.
    a. Note that on this map the word legend is used.
    b. Note the type of symbols which are used—lines, dots, numbers.

Summary

1. Question for the meanings of the three new words. Place these meanings on the board next to social studies (outlined in "Approach"). Have pupils note that the words legend and key have different meanings as used in social studies. Question for another meaning of key as used in social studies, "a small island." Have pupils note that the meaning of symbol does not change as used in mathematics or social studies.
2. Question: "Where is the legend or key generally placed in relation to the map? What were the different types of codes used on the maps we studied today?"
3. What steps did we take in using the coded information in the legend. As the steps are reviewed, place them on the map reading chart.
4. What information given in the legend did we not use today? State that the next lesson on map reading will be on how to use a scale of miles.

Exhibit VI

Lesson Outline for Organization

Skill:
Ability to organize and classify ideas.
Supplementary skill:
Introduction to outlining.

Approach (Motivation):
1. Refer to current season and tasks that confront mother. What does your mother mean when she says she has to organize her closets? Is the rest of your home organized in any fashion?
2. What kinds of organization do we have in a school (classes, grades, special groups)? Can organizing help us in our school work?
3. Present covers from *Time* Magazine. I am planning to save these covers for my social studies course. Shall I place them in one big pile, or is there a better way to file them? (Have students discuss how they would organize the pictures.)
4. We have worked with pictures and have organized them. Let us see if we can do the same with words.

Direct teaching techniques:
1. List words on chalkboard in scrambled order. Have students find words that belong together. Find main idea word for each group of words. List words under headings. Is there anyone who can remember all these items? What helped you remember?
2. From words, let us go to sentences. Distribute duplicated materials. Students select relevant facts.
   You are making a report on: "The important facts in the first United States space flight." Put an X near each sentence that you think is important for your report.
   a. The capsule was picked up in water.
   b. The flight took place at 10:00 A.M. on Friday, May 5, 1961.
   c. Commander Shepard has a lovely wife.
   d. It was a clear, beautiful day with little wind.
   e. Millions of people were worried about the flight.
   f. A Redstone rocket was used in the flight.
   g. The flight started from Cape Canaveral.
   Discuss reasons for omission of others.

Exhibit VI (*Continued*)

3. Proceed to sentences in paragraphs. What is the central thought? What are the details? How can we organize the details so as to be able to remember them?
4. Can we say the same thing in fewer words? Condense and paraphrase sentences. Present simple Harvard outline form.

Summary:
1. Class discussion and practice as to how to study a paragraph or chapter. Elicit:
   a. Read carefully.
   b. Select main idea.
   c. Select and organize supporting details, eliminating irrelevant facts.
   d. Write the outline form.
   e. Study the outline.

Follow-up:
1. Provide practice in:
   a. condensing sentences into topics by omitting unnecessary words
   b. changing order of words or making other changes to express the meaning of a topic
   c. distinguishing between topic and sentences
2. Provide practice in:
   a. selecting a main topic from a group of subtopics;
   b. composing a main topic from a group of subtopics;
   c. selecting from unsorted list of topics two which are the main topics. (List related subtopics under them.)
3. Provide practice in:
   a. finding details, subtopics when clue words are given
   b. finding subtopics in paragraph when events are given in sequence
   c. finding subtopics within paragraph when a comparison is made (advantages, disadvantages)

Mathematics

Mathematics requires a student to be a careful reader, able to read a problem, understand the specific technical language of mathematics, identify the question to be answered, see relationships, and distinguish relevant from irrelevant statements. He must be able to read graphs, equations, formulae, and tables and derive generalizations from these. Mathematics calls for highly specialized reading skills.

In order to be an efficient reader of mathematics, the student should be able to:

1. Understand specific vocabulary, word roots, symbols of mathematical operations, and spatial, temporal, quantitative relationships.
2. Solve problems which involve reading facts (details), seeing relationships (inference stated—not stated), estimating (predicting outcomes), testing results.
   a. Understand and use rules and definitions.
   b. Read critically.
   c. Follow directions.
   d. Understand sequence in operations.
3. Read and understand visual materials:
   a. Diagrams.
   b. Graphs.
   c. Geometric forms.
   d. Tables.

Exhibits VII, VIII, and IX give sample lessons in reading skill lessons integrated with mathematics content.

Exhibit VII

Lesson Outline in Mathematical Meanings

Skill:
Ability to note exact meaning of words used in mathematical contexts.

Approach (Motivation):
1. Show the following statement written on an elongated strip of paper: There are 70,000 words, but 1,000,000 meanings in our language.
2. Discuss the implications of this statement, pointing out that there are several meanings for some words.
3. Today we are going to work with some of those words in the math lesson, some of those which have special meanings in mathematics.

Direct teaching techniques:
Establish need for the knowledge of more than one meaning for some words by relating the story of a pupil who got into difficulty because he did not know the meaning of the word *check*.
1. Place across front ledge of board pictures or objects which pupils may use as basis of choice in clarifying meanings of words in the following sentences (sentences on chart):
   a. We need a *yard* of cloth.
   b. That line is a *foot* long.
   c. I used this *table* to find out what time my train would leave.
   d. We must know the *solution* for our math problems.
2. Elicit from pupils the special meaning as used in math for each of these words, and record them on a chart.

Summary:
Restate, with pupils, the importance of knowing the exact meaning of words as used in mathematical contexts.

Follow-up:
1. Suggested words for further study: bar, count, number, point, product, ruler, scale, square.
2. It is suggested that the teacher continue work on the above, and extend the list begun in this lesson. This list should be functional and cumulative.

Exhibit VIII

Lesson Outline in Mathematical Vocabulary

Skill:

Understanding the special vocabulary of Mathematics—developing the meaning of the word "percentage" through structural analysis (root words).

Approach (Motivation):

1. Display a picture of a centurion. Tell pupils this man is called a centurion. His title meant he was in charge of one hundred soldiers. Write meaning next to word.
2. Display newspaper ad with the word "centennial." Elicit from pupils what word would be of interest to us in this ad. Write the word centennial on the board under the word centurion. What do you notice about these two words? Have one pupil underline the "cent" in each word. Evoke from pupils what the word centennial could mean according to the ad (one hundred years). Write this on the board.
3. Bringing out some current or past aspect of the math work done by the class, elicit from them a word in math having "cent" in it. Elicit the word "percentage," or give the word if necessary.
4. Today we will learn the exact meaning of the word "percentage." Write this on the board.

Direct teaching techniques:

1. We have learned that "cent" means one hundred. Underline "cent" and write "one hundred" on the board.
2. Hand out two dictionaries. Have one pupil look up "per." Have the pupil give the dictionary meaning of "per" and write it on the board ("by"). Have another pupil look up "age." Do the same ("the act of").
3. Elicit from the pupils the meaning of the word "percentage" ("the act of dividing by one hundred").
4. Hold up a penny. Write on the board "one cent." Evoke from the students the exact meaning of "one cent" ("one, one hundred"). Elicit how they were able to get the meaning (from "cent = one hundred").
5. Write the word "centipede" on the board. What part of this word do we know? Have one pupil come to the board and underline "cent." Elicit meaning of one hundred. Develop PEDE. What word does this look like? ("PEDAL.") What do we use to pedal? ("Feet.") What do you think this word means? ("Insect with one hundred feet.")

Exhibit VIII (*Continued*)

Summary:
1. Review the value of knowing a root word.
2. Did we do what we set out to do? What helped us? (Knowing what "cent" means, dictionary, etc.) What did we learn? How can this skill help us? Can we use this skill in other classes? How? Where?
3. Have pupils set up section in notebook called "Math Vocabulary," and copy the word "percentage" and its meaning. Have pupils underline the root word "cent."

Follow-up:
1. Other mathematical words as developed to be added to the Math Vocabulary list and class chart. Root words should be underlined.
2. Develop the derivation of other words as they apply to math lesson and add to list.

Exhibit IX

Lesson Outline on Mathematical Comprehension

Skill:
Reading to solve problems; devising a plan to aid in sustaining the thought of the problem as a whole, and in finding the specific question asked.

Approach (Motivation):
1. Write on the board: . . . ___ . . .
   Does anyone know what I wrote on the board?
   Elicit answer: It is Morse Code meaning SOS ("Save our ship").
2. What is a code? Who uses code? Is it hard to break? Why? Evoke from pupils what some of these rules might be.
3. Did you know that we use a code in mathematics? Elicit some math symbols and write them on the board ($, %, ¢, etc.). Relate the math code to regular code. Steps must be followed to break the code.
4. Doing math problems means following steps, just as breaking a code means following steps.
5. Today we will learn some steps to follow to help us solve math problems.

Direct teaching techniques:
1. Present this math problem on the chalkboard: John has a bank account. He saves $12 a month. In 5 months he will spend ⅗ of his savings for a radio. How much money will he have left?
2. Before we can solve any problem what is the first thing we must do? Elicit answer: *Read the problem*. What is the purpose of this first reading? (*To understand vocabulary*.)

Exhibit IX (*Continued*)

Present Step 1 on a chart. Have pupils read silently. Have one pupil read it aloud. Why must we know all the words in a problem?

3. What do you think our next step is? Why is it necessary to *reread the problem?* (*To understand the whole problem.*) Present Step 2 on the chart. Explain to pupils that in this step they must keep in mind the *whole* thought of the problem, just as they keep (sustain) a note in music.
4. Have one pupil read the entire problem aloud. Elicit the next step. Present Step 3 on the chart. Have one pupil come to the board and underline the *question the problem asks.*
5. Can we do the problem now? (No.) Why not? Elicit Step 4. *What facts must we know in order to answer the question?* Have pupils take the problem apart sentence by sentence and have one pupil underline the facts. *Are the facts stated?* (Yes.) How do we know them? They are underlined. Are we ready to work now? (No.) Why? (*We need other facts.*) What facts must we *find?* (How much money John saved in 5 months.)
6. *Estimate* your answer; about how much money will John have left?
7. Do the problem.
8. Check your work; reread the problem to see if you have answered the question.

Summary:

What did we do? How can this help us? Have pupils copy the eight steps below in notebooks.

1. Read the problem . . . know all the words.
2. Read the problem again . . . for understanding. Keep the thought of the problem.
3. What question does the problem ask?
4. What number facts are given? Must we find other facts?
5. What process do we use? Do we add, multiply, subtract or divide?
6. Estimate the answer.
7. Do the problem.
8. Check your work. Reread the problem.

Follow-up:

1. Use chart to review steps and complete chart with class.
2. Use duplicated materials to fix the steps in problem solving.
3. Use textbooks for additional problems.

Note:

This is a developmental skill. It should be taken slowly step by step. Drill each step thoroughly. For *slow* learners, stop the lesson at Step 3. What question does the problem ask; drill at this point. For the very bright pupil, all the steps may be done at once.

Science

Science, like mathematics, requires slow, thoughtful, precise, analytical reading of detail. Experiments must be carried out through a step-by-step process. The student must read directions accurately, understand laws and principles, and know how to and when to apply them. Details of diagrams, formulae, and charts must be noted and relationships established. As have all content-area subjects, science has its own technical vocabulary and its own demands for problem solving. Can the student read the problem, identify the question or what is to be found, specify the facts that are given and those that are implied, form a hypothesis and then follow the steps necessary to arrive at a solution? Science is an accurate discipline and calls for exacting reading skills.

An efficient reader of science must be able to use the reading skills necessary to the scientific method of problem solving.

1. In order to identify and understand problems, the student must be able to:
   a. Understand the special and technical vocabulary of the field of science.
   b. Understand the general significance of the content of sentences, paragraphs, chapters.
   c. Understand how details of paragraphs, sentences, etc. support and illustrate the main idea.
2. In order to formulate hypotheses, the student must be able to:
   a. Organize ideas and understand relationships.
   b. Infer important ideas and relationships from data.
3. In order to collect information, the student must be able to:
   a. Differentiate fact from opinion, weigh evidence.
   b. Skim to locate specific information.
   c. Understand graphic and visual materials.
   d. Follow directions.
   e. Use research and library skills.
4. In order to test conclusions, the student must be able to:
   a. Recall information.
   b. Predict outcomes.

Exhibits X and XI are sample reading-skills lessons integrated with science content.

Exhibit X

Lesson Outline for Scientific Vocabulary

Skill:
Understanding special science vocabulary through the study of root words and drawing inferences.

Approach (Motivation):
1. There is something in this room that moves up and down. It is not alive. It moves very slowly. What is it? Give as many clues as necessary to elicit "thermometer."
2. Show the two types of thermometers, Fahrenheit and centigrade.
3. Today we are going to learn to make intelligent guesses as to the meanings of words which are unfamiliar to us.

Direct teaching techniques:
1. As the word "thermometer" is elicited, write it on the board. Advise that when scientists invent an instrument, a thermometer, for instance, they have to give it a name. How do you suppose they decided that this would be a good name for it?
2. Do you recognize any part of this word? Elicit "meter." What does it mean? (Measure.) The dictionary tells us that this word comes from the Greek word *metron* which means "measure." (Write on board.) Does the other part of the word look familiar to you? Do you know a word that looks something like this? Elicit "thermos bottle." What does a thermos do? (Keep warm.) What do you think this part of the word might mean? This also came from a Greek word, *therme*, meaning heat.
3. Fahrenheit (write on board) is a man's name. Can you guess why this thermometer (show Fahrenheit thermometer) should bear his name? (Inventor.)
4. Show the other thermometer. Do you know the name of this thermometer? Elicit "centigrade" (write on board). Let's see if we can discover why it is so named. Does any part of the word look familiar to you? Elicit "grade" and its meaning, "step." This comes from a Latin word, *gradus* meaning "step." Now look at the beginning of the word. What words do you know

Exhibit X (*Continued*)

that have "cent" in them? Elicit "century," "centennial," "per cent," and meanings. This is from the Latin word *centum* meaning "one hundred." What is the meaning of "centigrade"?

5. Distribute pictures of both types of thermometers. To which of these would you give the name centigrade? Why? Write the names of the thermometers in the blank spaces provided.

6. Look at the paper. Each line is a step. What do we call these steps? Elicit "degrees." Write on board. The dictionary tells us that "centigrade" and "degree" stem from the same Latin word, *degradare*, which is made from a prefix and a root word, *de* + *gradus*. What is the meaning of *gradus*? What is the meaning of *de*? Develop meanings of root and prefix.

7. What do we call this silvery substance? Show and elicit "mercury." Did you ever hear of a Greek god named Mercury? Who was he? Elicit "messenger of the gods." Is this a good name? Why?

8. Now we know the meanings of several root words. Point to "therm," "meter," "cent," and "grade." If you had to guess at the meanings of the words at the bottom of your paper, could you guess intelligently? Have pupils give approximate meanings. What helped you? If you needed an exact meaning what would you do? Elicit "Consult a dictionary."

Summary:

1. What have we learned? (Note the exact meanings of the above words through the use of roots and prefixes.)

2. Why should we be interested in learning the meanings of root words and their derivations?

Follow-up:

1. Add words to Vocabulary section of science notebook.

2. Add words to wall chart.

3. Have pupils find other words having the same root:
   a. thermostat, thermometer, etc.
   b. gradation, gradual, etc.
   c. altimeter, barometer, etc.

Exhibit XI

Lesson Outline in Reading a Scientific Diagram

Skill:
Reading diagrams.

Approach (Motivation):
1. Students examine picture and tell what purpose is served by pictures in a science textbook.
2. "In science, we use a special kind of picture, a diagram. Why is a diagram often more valuable to use in science than a picture? What must accompany a diagram so that we may understand it?"

Direct teaching techniques:
1. "Today, let's see if we can determine how to use a diagram efficiently." Examine a diagram of the voltaic cell. Note the names of the parts indicated in the diagram. Pupils try to name or label parts of the diagram after labels are removed. Remove labels from the diagram and then ask students to name the parts of the cell.
2. Distribute explanatory paragraphs for the diagram. Pupils read one sentence at a time. Look at the diagram. Relate each sentence to the parts of the diagram. Try to understand what happens as described in the sentence to each part of the diagram.
3. Have pupils try to explain in their own words the operation of the voltaic cell.
4. Have pupils analyze steps in reading a diagram. List on chalkboard:
   a. Study the diagram. Read the names of all the parts. Try to name the parts without reading them.
   b. Read the explanation, one step at a time. After each sentence, find the parts of the diagram mentioned. Try to understand what happens as described in the sentence.
   c. After reading the paragraph, try to tell in your own words what you have read.
   d. Reread the paragraph to be sure you have omitted nothing.

Summary:
1. Pupils review importance of skill studied.
2. Pupils copy into notebooks the points listed on the board under the heading "How to Read a Diagram."

Follow-up:
1. Pupils apply reading techniques to other diagrams.
2. Pupils practice drawing diagrams of things about which they read or experiments they have performed.

Industrial arts

Reading in an industrial arts and home economics program is a highly functional skill. This kind of reading is done by all members of a family, whether they have received an extensive or a limited education. Mother reads recipes, directions for using household appliances, thermometers, and labels on canned goods. Father reads bills, invoices, meters, directions for building home equipment and descriptions of the ways to use tools. The student, like the parent, has a practical interest in acquiring this skill and he applies it immediately. This is one of the reasons many industrial arts and home economics teachers find that they can be effective teachers of reading.

Identification of special terms, following directions, organization of facts or materials, reading of diagrams, are all special skills needed in shop areas. Caution must be used in the selection of reading material, as many pamphlets and books in the shop subjects are written in highly technical language. Attention should be given to the readability of materials. The *Reading Ease Calculator,* published by Science Research Associates in Chicago, gives a rough estimate of the difficulty of reading technical literature. A teacher in one of these areas would be wise to make a list of words most important to the subject, simplify directions and job specifications, and collect books and articles on different levels of difficulty so that all students would be able to have successful reading experiences. This procedure would greatly reduce frustration of poor readers and allow the class to move at a normal pace.

An efficient reader of industrial arts should be able to:

1. Understand and develop a vocabulary that will help him to identify tools, special equipment, utensils, common abbreviations and technical terms.
2. Follow directions, classify materials and processes
3. Read and interpret illustrations, diagrams and recipes.

Exhibits XII and XIII are sample reading-skills lessons integrated with industrial arts content.

Exhibit XII

Lesson Outline for Following Directions

Skill:
Following Directions

Approach (Motivation):
1. Tell the class you would like to learn where several things are kept in this shop (food shop).
2. Ask where you can find the measuring cup, the colander, the egg beater, and the cups and saucers. Follow the directions given and place these things on the table. Say to the class: What have I been doing? Elicit: "You have been following directions." What kind of directions have I been following? Elicit: "You have been following oral directions."
3. Give a pupil a card which reads: Go to the refrigerator and open the door. Take the butter from the refrigerator and place it on the table. Say to the class: How did this girl know what to do? Elicit: "She read it from the card." What was she really doing? Elicit: "She was following directions, written directions."

Direct teaching techniques:
1. What must we do if we wish to follow written directions?
2. Display a wall chart of directions for setting the table.
3. Have the students read the directions silently.
4. Have the directions reread aloud one at a time and the clue words underlined on the wall chart ("right," "left," "edge," "turned up," "left open," "side of bowl," "left of fork," "end of knife").
5. Have students close their eyes and visualize where to place utensils.
6. Have students come to front of room and place utensils in their proper places on the table.

Exhibit XII *(Continued)*

7. Have other members of the class prove that each direction has been correctly complied with by looking back at the directions and rereading each direction aloud.
8. Have a class secretary place a check after the direction on the chart if the object has been correctly placed on the table.

Summary:
What must we do if we wish to follow written directions?
1. We must read the directions carefully.
2. We must note the clue words which tell us what to do.
3. We must follow the directions exactly.
4. We must reread and check our directions to make certain we have not forgotten anything.

Follow-up:
1. Typed sheets of the table setting directions may be distributed, and the students may be asked to draw a picture of a place setting.
2. The following directions for making fruit gelatine may be given. The steps outlined above may be used by the class in following these directions.

Fruit Gelatine

Empty one box of lemon gelatine powder into a bowl. Pour two cups of hot water on the powder. Stir until the gelatine powder is dissolved. Peel one banana and two oranges. Slice them. When the gelatine starts to thicken, stir in the fruit and pour into a mold. Set the gelatine in the refrigerator to cool. Serve with one cup of whipped cream.

Exhibit XIII

Lesson Outline in Word Recognition

Skill:
To develop the ability to understand the special vocabulary used in shop.

Approach (Motivation):
1. Show class a newspaper advertisement for a carpenter's assistant. If you were to get the job what do you think you would have to do?
2. Here is a copy of a note you might get on the first day of your new job.
3. Show class a "blown-up" copy of the note. Elicit aim of the lesson from class by asking what they will need to know to answer the note. (We will learn the names of all the tools mentioned in the note.)
4. Have the enlarged carpenter's note read aloud: I am up on the tenth floor. Bring me the following tools:

mallet	pliers	gouge
chisel	coping saw	hammer
brace	hack saw	hand drill
bit	clamp	plane

Hurry.

Direct teaching techniques:
1. Using twelve individual word cards, have pupils match the word with its proper tool. See that all tools have been laid out on a work bench.
2. After all words have been matched, remove the tools. Tell class to remember the *use* for each tool. Ask class if they can see any words that could be grouped because they have a similar use. Continue questioning until *five* groups have been made:

mallet–hammer	pliers–clamp
chisel–gouge	brace–bit–drill
coping saw–hack saw–plane	

Summary:
How can this help you to be a good carpenter's assistant?

Follow-up:
1. Repeat steps 1 and 2 as often as needed in subsequent shop lessons. A concentrated effort will "fix" the basic sight vocabulary in each pupil's mind.

Evaluating the Program

As we have seen, skills of reading subject content differ from general skills used in reading. In each subject area, the student meets special difficulties. In order to assist the student, the teacher must determine how successful the student has been in acquiring the skills needed. By means of standardized or diagnostic tests, informal tests, and professional judgment, the teacher can discover the extent of a student's ability to function in reading tasks. No one test can indicate conclusively a student's ability to read. A comprehensive survey of all testing data should be considered in order to discover patterns in reading skills.

Standardized tests

Standardized-test scores in reading provide measures of a student's average reading ability. In specific reading skills, there is probably a considerable variation from the average score. A high ability in one skill may pull up the average score and give a false picture of one's reading ability. The reverse holds true when a student is poor in a particular skill; the average reading score could be depressed.

Most currently published tests limit themselves to a testing of a knowledge of the discipline itself and not to the unique skills necessary *for reading materials* in that discipline. However, some test makers have attempted (with limited success) to measure certain aspects of reading ability within the subject content. There is a great need for standardized tests in the various subject areas which measure more comprehensively a student's ability to read the content of the discipline. Such instruments would call for a new concept in standardized testing.

Despite the limitations of current tests in measuring ability to read in specific disciplines, the results of these instruments can be helpful in giving direction to a teacher, but cannot be considered as conclusive evidence of a student's ability to read content.

The following is a listing and brief description of some of the diagnostic measures that may be useful (with reservations stated above) in *specific* subject areas.

English language arts. Standardized tests in the English language arts are comprehensive and cover a number of reading skills. Most tests group the sub-tests into two major categories—vocalulary meaning and paragraph comprehension. In the *elementary grades* any number of standardized reading tests may be administered. A listing of these tests may be found in the *Mental Measurements Yearbook*.

Tests have also been devised to accompany certain basal reading programs. These tests, although not standardized, show pupil progress in specific materials studied, and measure some aspects of critical and creative reading.

For the *junior and senior high schools,* the following additional tests are recommended:

Cooperative Reading Test (Educational Testing Service)

This test is available in four forms on two levels: C_1 for junior and senior high schools and C_2 for upper high-school grades and college. It includes a number of items on literary appreciation.

ITED (Science Research Associates)

This test is available for grades 9 through 13. Test No. 3 is a test especially designed for the English language arts. It measures correctness and appropriateness of expression and tests the student on some of the basic elements in punctuation, usage, phraseology, and organization. Test No. 7 attempts to measure the understanding of high school pupils in reading literary material. It includes a number of selections from world literature, both prose and poetry, questions on understanding detail, direct and inferential comprehension of characterization; recognition of tone, mood, and emotion; recognition of the writer's viewpoint; understanding of imagery and figures of speech; a grasp of main thought or thoughts of passages, and an awareness of outstanding qualities of style and structure. Test No. 8 measures general ability in vocabulary, the ability to recognize the meaning of words commonly found in reading. Test No. 9 measures a student's ability to use the important sources of information such as: (1) a knowledge of the best procedures for turning to sources of information, (2) a knowledge of the purposes and nature of particular sources of information, (3) a knowledge of the specific content of the more common sources of information such as dictionaries, encyclopedia, and yearbooks, (4) the ability to interpret bibliographic references, and (5) the ability to use the card index.

Sangren-Woody Reading Test: Junior and Senior High School (Harcourt, Brace and World)

Part 7 tests ability to see the organization used by a writer.

STEP (Educational Testing Service)

This test is available on three levels: Level 3, grades 7 through 9; Level 2, grades 10 through 12; and Level 1, college. This test measures the ability to understand direct statements, interpret and summarize passages, discover motives of authors, observe organization of ideas, and criticize passages with respect to ideas and purpose of presentation.

The selections in the test are varied; they include directions and announcements, articles of information, letters, stories, poetry, articles of opinion and interpretation, and plays.

Social studies. The social studies tests which follow are among the better instruments for testing social studies concepts, but, again, they do not test exclusively the skill of *reading* social studies material. A student must have historical, economic, or geographical information in order to *read, understand,* and *answer* the questions.

Iowa Test of Basic Skills (Houghton-Mifflin Company)
Grades 3 through 9. Test W-1 measures ability in map reading. Test W-2 measures ability to read graphs and tables. W-3 measures the knowledge and use of reference materials.

ITED—Social Studies (Science Research Associates)
Test No. 5 measures the student's ability to interpret reading materials in social studies textbooks and references.

STEP—Social Studies (Educational Testing Service)
Level 4 (grades 4, 5, and 6); Level 3 (grades 7, 8, and 9); Level 2 (grades 10, 11, and 12); Level 1 (college). This test measures social studies understanding, the ability to read and interpret social studies material (maps, graphs, pictures), skills in seeing relationships among basic facts, trends, and concepts and the ability to analyze this material critically. Problems are drawn from all areas of social studies: history, geography, economics, government, sociology, etc.

Mathematics. While some test publishers make claims of testing the skills necessary for reading mathematics, it would be difficult to find questions which do not require understanding of the symbolic and quantitative language of mathematics. This reservation should be kept in mind in reading the following mathematics test recommendations:

Iowa Test of Basic Skills (Houghton-Mifflin Company)
Elementary and secondary. Test A-2 measures the ability to solve problems.

ITED—Mathematics (Science Research Associates)
Grades 9 through 12. Test No. 4 is a general mathematics test that attempts to measure the pupil's ability to do quantitative thinking.

STEP—Mathematics (Educational Testing Service)
Level 4 (grades 4, 5, and 6); Level 3 (grades 7, 8, and 9); Level 2 (grades 10, 11, and 12); Level 1 (college). This test measures the understanding of broad mathematical concepts, number and opera-

tions, symbolism, measurement, and geometry, function and relation, deduction and inference, probability, and statistics. Each level of the test deals with those concepts which mathematics educators feel should have been mastered by students at the various levels.

Tyler-Kimber Study Skills Test (Consulting Psychologists Press)

College level. This test measures advanced skills in the reading of mathematics.

Science. Tests in science generally demand a recall and understanding of specific science facts. Despite claims of some publishers, examination of sample test questions shows that the student must have a knowledge of the subject, in addition to the reading skills, if he is to obtain correct answers. Therefore, these instruments are *not* pure measures of a student's ability to read science material. It is well to bear this in mind when using the following test recommendations.

ITED—High School, Grades 9–12 (Science Research Associates)

Test No. 6 is designed to measure the student's ability to interpret and evaluate reading selections taken from science textbooks, reference material, scientific articles, in newspapers and periodicals, and from relatively non-technical popular scientific literature in general.

STEP—Science (Educational Testing Service)

Level 4 (grades 4, 5, and 6); Level 3 (grades 7, 8, and 9); Level 2 (grades 10, 11, and 12); Level 1 (college). This test measures the ability to identify and define scientific problems; to suggest or eliminate hypotheses; to interpret data and draw conclusions; to evaluate critically statements by others; and to reason quantitatively and symbolically. Questions are included in the areas of biology, chemistry, physics, meteorology, astronomy, and geology. The questions emphasize the application of science in home, economic, cultural, and social situations.

Informal (teacher-made) tests

The purpose of informal tests is to measure what has been learned against what has been taught in class. Informal or teacher-made tests, therefore, should be directly related to the material the student meets in his courses. This type of test can be given at any time as the lesson progresses: at the end of the lesson, at the end of a unit, or at the end of the term. Scores on such tests are usually limited to the number of correct responses. The only way teachers may compare the individual achievement of students is to build class norms.

Since the informal test is made by the teacher, its quality depends upon the skill and imagination of the individual teacher. Informal tests may be the result of group planning within a department or grade level. Perhaps each teacher may be made responsible for contributing test items. The entire group may then review the quetsions to make certain that the information required for answering the test items has been covered in each of the classrooms.

The classroom teacher should be acquainted with the principles of good test construction. Test items should be planned as the material is presented; they should measure information and skills relative to course objectives and should be specific to the type of information desired. Construction of a good test item takes time and should be planned for well in advance of the test. Brueckner and Bond [5] suggest different types of tests that can be used in an informal evaluation. These include problem situation tests, behavior records, inventories and questionnaires, analysis and evaluation of creative arts, sociometric procedures and evaluation of reactions using projective and expressive techniques.

Betts [6] discusses the general procedures in administering informal reading inventories and includes such items as the selection and organization of materials, how to check comprehension, working relationship between student and teacher in a test situation, how to estimate starting level, instructional level and frustration level, and how to record observation.

Strang [7] has outlined an informal guide for teachers that can be applied when observing a student's reading habits in *any* content area. The guide includes the following questions:

Was the relevant reading carried out with a clearly defined purpose?
Was the essential vocabulary understood?
Were the concepts comprehended?
Was there difficulty in applying comprehension abilities and study skills to the particular subject matter?
Was there difficulty in interpreting pictures, charts, graphs, tables, symbols, and abbreviations?
Was there proper adjustment in reading procedure to the specific organization of the subject matter?

[5] Leo J. Brueckner and Guy L. Bond, *The Diagnosis and Treatment of Learning Difficulties*, Appleton-Century-Crofts, New York, 1955.
[6] Emmet A. Betts, *Foundations of Reading Instruction*, American Book Company, New York, 1946, p. 456.
[7] Ruth Strang, materials developed at the Reading Center, Teachers College, Columbia University.

English language arts. Frank Perry recommends a diagnostic survey test of reading skills using a literature textbook. This can be applied to any textbook provided it is a well written book and that it can yield the information asked for in the test. Exhibit XIV gives the directions for constructing and administering this test.

Exhibit XIV

**Directions for Making and Administering
Diagnostic Survey Test of Reading Skills
Using an English Literature Textbook [8]**

I. Use between thirty-five and forty questions.
II. Use questions designed to measure the following reading skills in the proportions shown below.
   A. Using parts of a book (three questions in all). Include use of:
      1. Table of Contents.
      2. Index of Titles.
      3. Glossary.
      4. Biographical data.
      5. Introductory paragraph to story.
   B. Vocabulary needs:
      1. Meaning (seven or eight questions):
         a. General background of word meanings:
            i. Select correct meaning from several dictionary meanings.
            ii. Anonyms, synonyms.
         b. Contextual meanings.
      2. Word recognition and attack (fourteen or fifteen questions):
         a. Divided words into syllables.
         b. Designate the accented syllable.
         c. Note and give meaning of prefixes and suffixes.
         d. Changing the part of speech of a word (noun to verb, adjective to adverb, etc.).
   C. Comprehension (eleven or twelve questions):
      1. Noting the main idea.
      2. Recalling pertinent supporting details.
      3. Drawing conclusions, inferences.
      4. Noting the sequence of ideas.
   D. Reading Rate. Have pupil note the time it takes for him to read the selection. Then figure his reading speed in words per minute.

[8] Frank Michael Perry, "Helping Able Learners Improve Their Reading," unpublished doctoral thesis, Teachers College, Columbia University, 1961, pp. 134–135.

Exhibit XIV (*Continued*)

   E. Skimming to locate information (two to five questions).
III. Choose a reading selection of not more than three or four pages.
IV. In administering the inventory:
   A. Explain to the pupils the purposes of the inventory and the reading skills the inventory is designed to measure. As the inventory is given, let the pupils know the skill being measured.
   B. Read each question twice.
   C. Questions on the use of the parts of the book are asked first. Pupils will use their books.
   D. Introduce the reading selection, culling pupil background of experiences on the topic and setting up purpose questions.
   E. Selection read silently. Speed noted and figured.
   F. Ask questions on vocabulary. Pupils will use book for questions measuring ability to determine meaning from questions. All other vocabulary questions need to be written on the blackboard.
   G. Ask questions on comprehension. Pupils will not use books—books are to be closed.
   H. Skimming, new selection used. Pupils use book to find answers to questions.
   I. Survey, new selection used. Pupils survey and outline main points in limited time.
 V. A pupil is considered to be deficient in any one specific skill if he answers more than one question incorrectly, in an area measuring that specific skill.

The McCall-Crabbs test lessons [9] have attractive reading selections for students. Questions are asked at the end of each selection and grade scores are given. However, these grade scores are not dependable and should not be accepted as the student's reading level. The scores may serve as a motivating device for students and furnish a rough measure of a student's progress.

Social studies. A wide variety of reading skills are needed and the student should develop the ability to evaluate critically. Dressel and Mayhew list some of the critical abilities necessary to reading social studies materials. They caution that these abilities are not as distinct from one another as separate listing may seem to imply. In some prob-

[9] William A. McCall and Lelah Mae Crabbs, *McCall-Crabbs Standard Test Lessons in Reading*, Bureau of Publications, Teachers College, Columbia University, New York, 1961.

lems one uses a single skill; more complex problems may require the use of several skills. The following are the critical abilities referred to by Dressel and Mayhew: [10]

1. To identify central issues.
2. To recognize underlying assumptions.
3. To evaluate evidence or authority.
   a. To recognize stereotypes and clichés.
   b. To recognize bias and emotional factors in a presentation.
   c. To distinguish between verifiable and unverifiable data.
   d. To distinguish between relevant and non-relevant.
   e. To distinguish between essential and incidental.
   f. To recognize the adequacy of data.
   g. To determine whether facts support a generalization.
   h. To check consistency.
4. To draw warranted conclusion.

A short answer form for students to use in evaluating their own ability to think critically has also been developed by Dressel and Mayhew. This form appears here as Exhibit XV. Although intended for the secondary level, teachers of elementary school children will also find helpful suggestions in this guide.

[10] Paul L. Dressel and Lewis B. Mayhew, *Critical Thinking in Social Science,* William C. Brown, Dubuque, Iowa, 1954.

Exhibit XV

A Short-Answer Form for Evaluating
Critical Thinking in Social Science [11]

You will be given an opportunity to read and study a passage of social science writing, and to give your interpretation of it. Read through all the questions to see what is expected of you before beginning.

In the various questions which follow, you will be asked to examine the selection from several points of view. You may answer the questions in any order. There will probably be more things to note under some questions than others, but you should make your coverage as complete as possible.

1. List any stereotypes or clichés which you can find in the selection.
2. List any examples you can find of emotional or biased statements in the selection.
3. Does the selection present unverifiable data as though they were facts? If so, list them.
4. What is the main point in this selection?
5. Are the facts which are presented in the selection as supporting the author's position pertinent to his argument? Explain.
6. What additional information is needed ·before passing judgment upon the author's position? Or, do you think enough data have been provided?
7. Is the presentation consistent? If not, list examples of inconsistencies.
8. Judging the selection as a whole, what are some of the ideas and beliefs which the author takes for granted?
9. What thoughts and feelings on the general subject did you have before you read the passage which may have influenced your reaction to the selection?
10. What are *your own* conclusions with respect to the main point of the selection?

(*Note:* If this form is reproduced for student use, space should be left between questions in which students will write their responses.)

Mathematics. It is particularly important in mathematics to administer a test as soon as new material is introduced. If errors are made, the more time that elapses between the error and the correction, the more the likelihood exists that incorrect concepts will be fixed.

[11] Dressel and Mayhew, *op. cit.,* p. 12.

A teacher-made test in mathematics might include the following types of questions:

1. Special vocabulary: Use the following words in sentences as they would be used in mathematics.

plane	surface
triangle	degree
angle	area

2. Structural analysis: What is the meaning of the prefix "geo"? What is the meaning of the suffix, "metry"? Give a definition of the word "geometry."

3. Reading a problem: The teacher presents a problem for which the solution is not required. The teacher might ask the following questions:

   a. What is asked for in this problem?

   b. List the facts needed in solving the problem?

   c. What method of computation will you use in solving this problem? (If more than one, list the processes in order.)

   d. How can you test to see if the answer is reasonable and accurate?

4. How to read symbols:

The teacher presents a series of diagrams and the pupils decide which figures have the same size and shape and which figures differ in size and shape. For example:

$$\triangle \qquad \triangle$$
$$\circ \qquad \bigcirc$$

The teacher asks questions to determine if the pupil understands the meaning of terms represented by symbols or abbreviations. For example:

÷ stands for:

qt. stands for:

Another way of testing a student's knowledge of symbols or abbreviations is to list the symbols in one column and the meanings in a second column. The pupil draws lines to match the symbol with its meaning.

Science. Dressel and Mayhew have developed a guide for a student to use in reading and analyzing a science selection, which appears here as Exhibit XVI. It includes questions which reveal the ability to identify problems, locate and evaluate information, to formulate hypotheses and to draw conclusions. The teacher, with this information, may then plan a reading program on the basis of the answers given in the guide.

Exhibit XVI

Student Guide (Instructions) [12]

A. *Read* the article you have selected thoroughly, two or three times.
B. *Analyze* the method or methods used in attacking the problem as revealed in the article. This is sometimes difficult to do in a popularly written scientific article, where the author frequently glosses over the different steps and endeavors to glamorize the results beyond what the scientist would do. Before you can start writing you will have to ferret out these steps for yourself. The following points may be helpful to you in your thinking:
   1. *The problem:*
      a. What is the primary problem with which the article is concerned?
      b. Is it a fairly small, isolated problem or part of a still larger problem?
      c. What motivated the scientist or group of scientists to attack the problem?
   2. *The hypotheses:*
      a. What hypotheses, explicit or implied, are considered in the pursuit of the problem?
      b. Was any hypothesis directly inferred from some of the relevant facts?
      c. Are the hypotheses tentative or are they part of some conceptual scheme which has already had considerable support?
   3. *The factual material or data:*
      a. How much factual information was at hand before the problem was recognized or attacked?
      b. How were further data on the problem obtained? By observation? By controlled experiment?
      c. Were deductive tests of any hypotheses designed and carried out? Did they lead to revisions in the hypothesis being tested?
   4. *The results:*
      a. How successfully was any hypothesis supported by the results of the investigation?
      b. Could the results be confirmed by others who wished to check the work?
      c. To what extent were personal interpretations involved in the results? Is there any indication of prejudice or bias?
      d. Were important aspects of the problem neglected?

[12] Paul L. Dressel and Lewis B. Mayhew, *Science Reasoning and Understanding*, William C. Brown Company, Dubuque, Iowa, 1954, p. 64.

Exhibit XVI (*Continued*)

   e. In the light of your limited knowledge of the subject, what further studies might be made to reinforce the results?

C. *Evaluate* the reporting of the problem by the author of the article.

   1. To what extent did the author try to show the nature of the problem and the efforts at its solution?

   2. How faithfully did he try to portray variant points of view?

   3. Was he authoritarian or dogmatic in his reporting?

   4. To what extent was his treatment unconvincing or lacking in important steps?

Reading of subject content begins in the primary grades and becomes more important as the child progresses into the intermediate and secondary grades where the material becomes more specialized. To evaluate a student's ability to read subject content, one can use either standardized or informal tests or a combination of both. Perhaps in subject fields (because of the inadequacy of standardized tests in this area) informal procedures such as teacher made tests are better indications of a student's needs and growth.

Once a student has become a competent reader of subject content, each curriculum field can serve as a springboard for the expansion of reading interests. Efficient reading content materials, like all reading, has as its objective, the intellectual development of the individual.

Suggested Reading

Bamman, Henry A., Ursula Hogan, and Charles E. Green, *Reading Instruction in the Secondary Schools*, New York, Longmans, Green, 1961, Chapters VII through XII.

Brownell, John Arnold, "The Influence of Training in Reading in the Social Studies on the Ability to Think Critically," *California Journal of Educational Research*, IV (January 1953), 28–31.

Five Steps to Reading Success in Science, Social Studies and Math, Metropolitan School Study Council, New York, 1960.

Improving Reading in All Curriculum Areas, Supplementary Education Monographs, University of Chicago Press, Chicago, November 1952.

Improving Reading in the Content Fields, Supplementary Education Monographs, University of Chicago Press, Chicago, January 1947.

Improving Reading in the Junior High School, Department of Health, Education and Welfare, Bulletin #10, Government Printing Office, Washington, D. C., 1957.

Peterson, Eleanor, *Aspects of Readability in Social Studies,* Bureau of Publications, Teachers College, Columbia University, New York, 1954.

Shephard, David L., *Effective Reading in Science,* Row, Peterson, Evanston, Ill., 1960.

————, *Effective Reading in Social Studies,* Bureau of Publications, Teachers College, Columbia University, New York, 1954.

Spache, George D., "Types and Purposes of Reading in Various Curricula Fields," *Reading Teacher,* II (February 1958), pp. 158–64.

Swerkin, E. H., "A Basic Vocabulary and Glossary in Machine Tools," *Industrial Arts and Vocational Education,* 48 (March 1959), pp. 104–108.

Williams, S. L., and S. A. Anderson, "Power of Words in Industrial Arts," *American Vocational Journal,* 27 (December 1952), p. 12.

3   Flexible Grouping in Reading Instruction

Educators are constantly appraising instructional practices and policies, making modifications where necessary to meet the changing needs of students and of changing curricula. However, some aspects of the instructional complex have become so firmly imbedded in the matrix of the educational process that they no longer receive the critical scrutiny they deserve.

Should we not consider possible variation of group size for the purpose of differentiating instruction? Are we to continue to assume that all children learn in classes of thirty, or do some have more successful experiences in large groups while others need small group or individual instruction?

Not only has the size of the class been limited, but many schools have been built to accommodate a maximum of thirty-five seats in the classroom. The exceptions have been the auditorium, the library, and the school cafeteria. We say, in effect, that large numbers of children can assemble in the school auditorium, eat together in a lunch room, and use the facilities of the school library, but they cannot have a common learning experience together. We say this despite the fact that we are aware of the educational value of television, radio, and films for large numbers of an unseen audience.

Once the issue of class size has been raised, many interesting questions arise. Is it possible that schools have been neglecting a profitable avenue of learning by not providing for flexible grouping in instruction? Can some students learn in large lecture groups as well as in conventionally sized classes? Do other students learn more effectively in small groups? Can some students learn independently? Can students be more stimulated by association with large numbers of students and with more than one teacher? Should special talents of exceptional teachers be shared with as many students as possible? Can time be found within the school day to lighten teachers' instructional programs so that they have more time to meet in groups, prepare lessons, develop imaginative materials, and keep up to date professionally? Will pooling of teacher ideas and observations lead to better teaching? A search for the answers to these questions is, in essence, the guiding principle for experimentation in flexible programing.

Once the concept of large and small groups is accepted, we find that certain forms and methods of instruction—such as team teaching, television, films, slides, language laboratories, and self-selection programs —are readily adaptable to such groupings. For this reason, these instructional devices are discussed in this chapter.

The Teaching Team in Flexible Grouping

One of the newer approaches to flexible grouping for instruction is combining students for large and small group lessons under the direction of a team of teachers.

Dr. J. Lloyd Trump, director, under a Ford Foundation grant, of a project to study staff utilization in secondary schools, states: "Some aspects of learning will be presented by especially qualified teachers to relatively large groups of students. This, in turn, will provide more opportunities for students to explore ideas in small discussion groups and in independent activities. Although some classes will be much larger, paradoxically the student will assume more individual responsibility for learning." [1]

When Dr. Trump speaks of "some aspects of learning," it becomes relevant to ask, "can reading become one of them?" Until recently, it has been our assumption that, the smaller the reading group, the more effective the learning. Is it not possible that the converse, too, may have some merit? May we not assume that, in some instances of selected reading lessons, students in large groups have more effective learning experiences than those in conventionally sized groups? Experimentation and research in schools throughout the country indicate that this is possible. The Newton, Massachusetts, school system presents lessons in the appreciation skills to four tenth-grade classes at a time. In Pittsburgh, four second-grade classes receive basic-read-

---

[1] J. Lloyd Trump, *Images of the Future*, National Association of Secondary School Principals, Washington, D. C., 1959, p. 7.

ing-skills lessons twice a week. Both school systems have found this method effective and are extending their program. In the Franklin School in Lexington, Masachusetts, the personnel has been reorganized into four teams. Reading and arithmetic are taught in grades one through six to groups of students ranging from five to 215 in a group. This program, established in 1958, is continuing with extensive experimentation in teacher and pupil redeployment.

The concept of combining classes for instruction under a single instructor began in the secondary schools. Since large group instruction was patterned after the college lecture courses, it was thought that only very bright youngsters in the secondary school could benefit from this approach. The program was aimed, generally, at those students who would eventually enter college. Subsequently, a concern for gifted students at the elementary level prompted experimentation there, as well.

Upon re-examination of the original educational objectives, leaders recognized that most students could benefit from "master teaching" in large groups. This approach was then extended to able and less able students in both elementary and secondary schools.

In New York City, four seventh-grade classes became part of a program of team teaching. Reading was selected as the area of instruction in this project because the school chosen for the experiment was located in a disadvantaged community and had many poor readers among its students. Each week a group of 120 students reported to the auditorium for a lesson in basic reading skills. The follow-up lesson was given in the regular classroom. Those students who had difficulty in mastering the skills were given small-group instruction, and some met individually with a teacher. Small-group and individual instruction was possible because the school was willing to break conventional schedule patterns. The program is now being extended to other subject areas because the staff and the students were enthusiastic about the opportunity to participate in a variety of group patterns.

It should be noted that scheduling the hard-to-achieve small groups will be possible whenever a way is found to successfully teach a large group. Although small-group leadership requires a different type of competency than does large-group instruction, both types of abilities are essential. Therefore, each team should include "master teachers" of both small and large groups.

The following are some of the numerous advantages that flexible grouping holds for teachers and students.

Advantages for the student

1. Enrichment of pupil learning through master lessons presented by gifted teachers.

2. The opportunity of small-group and individual instruction. In periods where several classes meet for instruction by one teacher, the other teachers are available to meet small groups for more specialized reading help.

Advantages for the teacher

1. Enabling of teachers with special talents, interests, and activities to share them with more students than is possible in the conventionally sized classroom.

2. Opportunity for staff members who are unfamiliar with or inexperienced in methods of teaching reading to observe master lessons.

3. More preparation time for teachers, which enables them to plan more effective lessons.

In the consideration of new approaches to grouping for instruction, experiments now in progress should be studied. The National Association of Secondary School Principals of the National Education Association of Washington, D. C., is a resource organization offering information about current experimentation in team teaching. Individual school systems are always willing to share their plans of organization with representatives of other school systems. Philadelphia and Pittsburgh, Pennsylvania; Evanston, Illinois; Newton, Massachusetts; St. Louis, Missouri; and New York City are among the school systems that are active in experimentation of this type.

Setting Up the Teaching Team

The composition of the teaching team will vary with each program. The following is but one example of a teaching team and can be used as a guide to an over-all structure.

The team leader

This person is a master teacher and is responsible for *coordinating and directing* all activity of the team members and the students in the group. In some school systems, there is supplementary remuneration for the position. By creating the position of team leader, we not only give master teachers recognition and salary increment, but we place a premium on retaining quality teaching in the classroom.

The team leader combines classroom teaching and supervision. He has the dual role of being a master teacher to the large number· of students under his direction and a guiding supervisor to the members of his team. He, with the other members of the team, prepares the lessons, practice materials, and tests. With the help of participating teachers, student teachers, and a technician (if available), he prepares the instructional materials. Very often these materials are more elaborate than those used in the conventional classroom, as they must be highly motivating, legible to large audiences and, if on discs or tapes, clearly audible.

In addition to these activities, the team leader meets in conferences with the participating teachers to plan the next large-group lesson and the follow-up lessons. His weekly schedule should provide time for visiting the classrooms of the participating teachers to assist in the follow-up lessons. Because of the many responsibilities of the position, it is recommended that the team leader teach no more than five large groups per week. Conferences, preparation of materials, and follow-up lessons occupy the remaining periods of a team leader's weekly schedule.

Participating teachers

These are the teachers of the classes that make up the large instruction groups. They are responsible for the follow-up lessons in their own classrooms. Some of the participating teachers may assist in certain aspects of the large-group lessons, others may be assigned to work with small groups, and still others may be team leaders in other aspects of the English language arts. No matter what assignments the participating teacher has, he attends the follow-up conference with the team leader in order to be able to plan the next lesson that will be given in his classroom.

In some programs, the team leader himself gives a demonstration lesson in the participating teacher's classroom to follow the large-group instruction. In other programs, the follow-up lessons are given by the participating teacher. He may invite the team leader into the room to observe the lesson and submit lesson plans for suggestions. Although the team leader assists wherever possible, responsibility for classroom teaching remains with the participating teacher.

Observing teachers

These teachers do not have classes taking part in the large-group instruction, but they observe the lesson in order to learn more about the teaching of reading. Very often they are new teachers or ones with new assignments. Observing a lesson becomes more meaningful if teachers know what to look for. The guide appearing in Exhibit I may help to make their observations more productive. (This guide may be used by anyone observing the lesson: new teachers, participating teachers, supervisors, and student teachers.)

Exhibit I

Observers' Guide for Large-Group Instruction

Date: _____ Subject area: _____
Approximate instructional level: _____
Classes: 1. _____ 2. _____ 3. _____ 4. _____
Team-leader: _____ Participating teachers: _____

	Yes	No
I. Physical Arrangements		
A. Use of available space		
1. Does each student have a seat?	_____	_____
2. When seats are not on graduated level, does the teacher have a raised platform?	_____	_____
3. Are instructional materials set up by the time the lesson begins?	_____	_____
4. Does the room lend itself to the decentralization of visual material?	_____	_____
5. Is writing space provided for: desk arms, tablets, clip boards?	_____	_____
6. Is there space for books which students may be carrying?	_____	_____
7. Are the seats comfortable and the proper size for the students?	_____	_____
B. Seating plan		
1. Does the seating configuration vary with the needs of the lesson (V-shape, semi-circle, straight rows, alternating seats)?	_____	_____
2. Are students with handicaps or special problems seated appropriately?	_____	_____
C. Lighting conditions		
1. Are there window shades?	_____	_____
2. Has natural light been properly controlled to prevent glare?	_____	_____
3. Is the artificial lighting adequate?	_____	_____
4. Are there darkening facilities in the room?	_____	_____

Exhibit I (*Continued*)

	Yes	No
E. Sound conditions		
1. Are distracting noises eliminated?	_____	_____
2. Can children hear in all parts of the room?	_____	_____
3. Is there provision for amplification of teacher and student voices?	_____	_____
4. When phonographs or tape recorders are used, is there provision for extension speakers and proper amplification?	_____	_____
F. Ventilation		
1. Is there provision for adequate air circulation?	_____	_____
2. Is temperature properly controlled?	_____	_____
II. Development of the Lesson		
A. Objective—is it clear?	_____	_____
B. Motivation or approach		
1. Are the motivational activities appropriate to the lesson?	_____	_____
2. Is the length of time spent on motivation adequate?	_____	_____
C. Sequence—is the sequence of the lesson logical?	_____	_____
D. Timing and interaction		
1. Is sufficient time given to each step in the lesson?	_____	_____
2. Are pupils given time to react to statements and ideas?	_____	_____
3. Is there some opportunity for participation?	_____	_____
4. Is there a medial summary?	_____	_____
5. Is there a final summary?	_____	_____
E. Application		
1. Are there reinforcement practices?	_____	_____
2. Are follow-up assignments clear?	_____	_____
F. Evaluation		
1. Is provision made for informal evaluations?	_____	_____
2. Is provision made for student reactions to lessons?	_____	_____

Exhibit I *(Continued)*

	Yes	No
III. Instructional Materials		
A. Appropriateness of content		
1. Is the subject matter of instructional materials appropriate to the lesson?	___	___
2. Is the vocabulary familiar to the student?	___	___
3. Are the concepts within the experiential background of the students?	___	___
4. Are the facts accurate and current?	___	___
B. Physical qualities		
1. Are charts legible?	___	___
2. Are the materials attractive?	___	___
3. Is there sufficient detail without clutter?	___	___
4. Are the visuals large enough to be seen by all students in the room?	___	___
5. Is sound clear and audible?	___	___
C. Variety—does the teacher use a variety of materials: chalkboard, overhead projectors, flannelboard, records, phonographs, films, charts, textbooks, etc.?	___	___
D. Planning and use—are materials arranged in a convenient, logical order so the teacher has immediate access to them?	___	___

Student teachers

Student teachers are often assigned to the large-group instruction program for purposes similar to those of the observing teachers. Extra periods during the school day may be assigned to these students so they may assist the team leader or the technician in the preparation of charts, slides, and tapes. The student teacher who is interested and competent may be asked to present parts of a lesson. It is from the student teachers that the team leader develops future participating teachers and, eventually, team leaders.

More and more, teacher-training institutions are including opportunities for student teachers to observe and participate in large-group instruction. For example, the School of Education of New York University assigned one of its classes in the methods of teaching English language arts to attend a weekly large-group lesson in reading in a New York City junior high school. Several of these students, upon graduation, asked for assignment to this school in order to take part in its program.

The Harvard University School of Education assigns third- and fourth-year students to the large-group teaching program in the Newton, Massachusetts, public school system. Again, a number of these student teachers elect to enter that system in order to continue their participation in large-group instruction. In the Glenbrook High School in Northbrook, Illinois, an internship program is an integral part of the team teaching pattern.

Teacher assistants

These are paraprofessional aides who, along with professional teachers, assist in specific aspects of team teaching. They correct test papers, check notebooks, help in preparation of materials, and perform routine clerical duties such as typing stencils and recording grades. Many school systems do not now provide teacher assistants, but this should not deter a school from reorganizing for flexible grouping. However, through the use of teacher assistants, it will be possible to fully "professionalize" teaching and release the teacher from peripheral duties. Arlington High School and Prospect High School in Arlington Heights, Illinois, use instructional assistants in all their programs. Jefferson County, Colorado, employs instructional and clerical assistants in eight of its high schools.

Mobility within the team

Flexible grouping should allow not only for mobility of students, but for movement within the teaching team as well. A participating teacher, after a given period of time, may be ready to give a large group lesson in preparation for moving into the role of a team leader. An observing teacher may ask that his class be invited to participate in the next large-group topic. A student teacher may be capable of presenting part of a large-group lesson. A team leader will know when to suggest that teaching positions change within the team. The success of this program rests not only on its organization and instructional quality, but on the leadership qualities of the team leader and on the interests and competencies of the professional staff.

Selecting the Team Pattern

The choice of a pattern of organization for flexible grouping will depend on the particular objectives of the program, the classes selected and the quality and experience of the teaching personnel. All concerned should study the many possible organizations carefully before making a decision. The following are examples of organization patterns.

Pattern 1: Participating teachers given other assignments

Personnel consists of a team leader, observing teachers, and student teachers. In this organization all the teachers of the classes attending the large-group lessons (participating teachers) are competent in the teaching of reading. These teachers know how to proceed on their own; it is not necessary for them to observe the lesson. They may be given other teaching assignments during the large-group lessons. Because the participating teachers are free for other assignments, such as small-group lessons and discussions, this pattern permits greater variation in group size. However, it is recommended only if all the participating teachers are skilled in the teaching of reading.

In this plan, the follow-up lesson is given by the participating teacher in his own classroom, even though he has not observed the large-group lesson. He is able to do this because he has spoken to the team leader in conference and, with him, has planned the follow-up lesson. This pattern can be varied so that the team leader gives the follow-up lesson in each participating teacher's classroom. Thus, the need for a conference is eliminated and sequential teaching is assured. This is the practice in Pittsburgh where the social studies and English teachers teach those subjects only, to all the students in both large and small group situations. However, it is not recommended that the team leader be the sole teacher of reading. Since reading is a skill needed in all study—a skill that is best learned in subject context—it is important that all teachers know how to teach reading and that reading be taught as an integral part of every subject.

Pattern 2: Team leader in training

In this pattern there are: a team leader, participating teachers, observing teachers, and student teachers. One of the participating teachers is in training to take the position of a team leader for either this group or for another large group. He observes the lessons, helps in preparing materials and is gradually given the opportunity of presenting lessons to the large group. This "team leader in training" may eventually alternate with the regular team leader or may take over a group of his own. The other teachers of the classes that are part of the large group assume other assignments, such as teaching small groups or being team leaders for other large group meetings.

As in Pattern 1, a weekly conference may be held by the team leader for all the participating teachers, whether or not they are present at the lesson. Since in this organization, all the teachers are skilled, each participating teacher plans her own follow-up lesson under the guidance of the team leader. Student teachers are included in every phase of the large-group organization. It is recommended that in this plan student teachers be invited by the classroom participating teachers to observe and present some of the follow-up lessons. This gives the student teacher practice in conventional classroom instruction as well as large-group instruction.

Pattern 3: Participating teachers attend

This pattern includes a team leader, participating teachers, observing teachers, and student teachers. All the teachers of the participating classes attend the large-group lesson (whereas in Pattern 1, none did, and in Pattern 2, only the "team leader in training" did). The purposes of this plan are (1) teacher education and (2) improvement of pupil instruction through the use of master teachers. When this plan is used, it is assumed that the staff is new and inexperienced and needs an opportunity to observe a well-structured and well-developed reading lesson. The team leader gives each participating teacher a copy of his lesson plan so that he can follow the development of the lesson. In addition, he may be given the Observation Guide suggested in Exhibit I of this chapter.

The follow-up lessons given in the several classrooms are planned by the team leader and the participating teachers in conference. The team leader should be present in the classrooms when these follow-up lessons are given. He helps in planning the lesson and offers suggestions for improvement after observing the lesson. At no time does he assume the role of a rating officer.

Pattern 3, although useful in teacher training, leaves little or no room for varying the sizes of groups, since all classes are combined into one large group, and all the teachers are involved in observing the large-group lesson. However, as the school year progresses, one or two participating teachers may develop sufficient skill to assume some small-group instruction. When the participating teacher does assume small-group instruction, it is important that she be given as much guidance in the preparation of her lessons in this situation as she has been given for large-group instruction.

Selection of Groups

Attempts should be made to select classes having similar ranges in reading ability. The range should be confined to a maximum span of three years. Students below and beyond these limits will probably not benefit from the large-group lesson. In the secondary schools, large reading groups should be chosen from the English language arts and social studies classes where the teaching of reading skills is an important objective. It is a good idea, whenever possible, to create two large-group classes—one for normal and bright youngsters and another for students with reading disabilities.

A large group may include classes from three different grades, all with a reading range, for example, of 4.8 to 6.2 and with a median reading score in the fifth grade. One class may be a bright fourth grade, the second a normal fifth grade, and the third a slow sixth grade. This type of ungraded scheduling may create minor problems in terms of what to read (as each grade has its own curriculum requirements). However, in all grades there are common concepts that can be taught and the teaching team should seek to identify them.

Other patterns for selection might be considered. Students with common interests and abilities can be grouped without regard for grade levels or class placement. Students may also be grouped on the basis of one criterion for mathematics instruction and another for reading instruction in other subject disciplines.

Special abilities and disabilities of students can also be accommodated in flexible grouping by withdrawing them from the large group and giving them the opportunity of having the guidance of a teacher in small groups.

However, placing students in the appropriate groups is a problem that will always require flexible and tentative solutions. Which children learn best in large groups, which in small groups? When do you move youngsters from one group to another? Do all children adjust to several teachers or do some children need the security of a single teacher? These are just a few questions that can be raised about pupil deployment.

Scheduling Classes

In the secondary schools

Two or more classes may be scheduled to meet at the same period. One may be a class in history and the other a class in English. In this way, the teacher of either subject may present materials to both sections, combining them to save time and effort. This is commonly called "back-to-back scheduling." An example is seen in Exhibit II.

Exhibit II

"Back-to-Back Scheduling"[2]

Period	Regular Schedule		Combined
	English Miss X	History Mr. Y	Either Miss X or Mr. Y
1	Section A	Section B	Sections AB
2	Section B	Section A	Sections AB

Another way of scheduling is to parallel two or more English language arts classes so they meet at the same time each day. You may choose to have them meet as a single section twice a week and meet in the conventionally sized classes for the remainder of the week. When they meet as a single section, the teachers other than the team leader may be assigned to work with smaller groups—some pupils may need remedial help, and others may need to be freed to work outside the scope of the regular course of study.

Although each participating teacher may have a different assignment, the teachers should be programed to meet for a common conference with the team leader. The conference period is an integral part of team teaching. It affords the participating teachers (teachers of the classes that combine for large-group instruction) an opportunity to plan the sequence of lessons to be taught in their own classrooms; to report on the success of these follow-up lessons and to make suggestions for future large-group experiences. The team leader uses this information as a guide in his planning. The conference period is an invaluable

[2] J. Lloyd Trump, *Images of the Future,* National Association of Secondary School Principals, Washington, D. C., 1959, p. 43.

aid to new teachers who, through these discussions where follow-up lessons in the classroom are planned, can follow the sequential development in the teaching of reading skills.

In elementary schools

Elementary schools present a different problem in programing since, in most instances, there are no changes of periods and no subject specialists. The elementary school teacher is a generalist and is expected to be able to teach all subjects. Is this not too much to expect? It would seem that almost every teacher would excel in some specific area. A teacher's area of superior ability should be shared by more students than would normally be seated in a conventionally sized classroom.

In Pittsburgh, a team of primary teachers is organized for each of the first three grades. This team consists of teacher specialists in reading, speech, and English language arts. For all other subjects the children are assigned to a single classroom teacher. Pupil assignments to the individual teachers within the team vary, depending on specific requirements and the extent of progress. For example, the team member who specializes in reading instruction might give special help to a group of seventy-five children found to be lacking in a particular skill. Another twenty-five pupils, who, upon pre-testing, are found not to need this particular skill, might be divided into two small groups with two teachers who would work with them in composition and give corrective instruction in speech. These twenty-five students will meet with the reading teacher specialist at another time during the day to study either more advanced skills or to discuss other problems they may have encountered in their reading. Members of the original group of seventy-five students will meet in small groups at other times during the week with the reading specialist, the teacher of speech and the English language arts teacher. The distinctive feature of this plan is the assignment of large groups of pupils to a group of teachers rather than the allotment of a fixed number of pupils to a single teacher.

In the intermediate grades, the pattern is extended to include all major content subjects—English language arts, social studies, mathematics, and science. The English language arts and social studies are combined and taught by teacher specialists. These specialists have the complete responsibility of teaching their subjects to grades four, five, and six. The same pattern is applied to mathematics and science with specialists responsible for those subjects in grades four, five, and six.

The teacher specialists are assigned to the entire fourth grade and the lower half of the fifth grade in the morning, and to the upper half of the fifth and the entire sixth grade in the afternoon. In this type of "ungraded" scheduling, lower-grade students can move into the afternoon class as soon as they are ready to join a more advanced group, and upper grade students who are not achieving can move into the morning group where they have an opportunity to review skills they may not have learned.

The teaching specialists within the different content areas become a team similar to the team established in the primary grades. Because a group of students is assigned to a team of teachers rather than a single teacher, class size becomes flexible and students are able to receive help in small groups.

Encouraging the Students to Participate

In the teaching of a large group, the lecture type presentation is most frequently used, but this does not preclude student participation. In large-group lessons, student participation may take forms other than recitation, such as listening and note taking. In Newton, Massachusetts, these skills are taught by the team leader as initial lessons.

Another form of student participation is for the teacher to ask a student to read a passage or organize reading materials for classification of facts. He may use a skill sheet that will call upon the student to circle, underline, or supply the information.

Students can be asked to make slides, charts, film cuts, and overlays that are needed in the lesson. Participation may take many forms, and an imaginative team leader will involve the students throughout the lesson.

Planning

The time for planning is in a preliminary workshop. Since reading skills do not stand apart from the curriculum, a plan for integrating the large-group lesson into the course of study should be evolved before the start of the term.

As with all planning, changes may become necessary as the lessons proceed. Students may not be able to keep the pace set by the instructor, or they may be able to progress at a much faster pace. Adjustments should, of course, be made as soon as the need is noticed.

Exhibit III is a sample of a twelve-week plan of instruction in reading, which includes large-group instruction and suggested follow-up lessons in the classroom. This is just one of many possible sequences.

Exhibit III

Sample of a Twelve-Week Reading Plan

Classes: 7¹, 7², 7³, and 7⁴.　　　　　Reading range: Levels 4 through 6.

Number of sessions: Depends upon how effective large-group approach is to lesson.

Length of period: Depends upon school schedules (minimum, 30 minutes; maximum, a full hour).

Week number and area of study	Large-group lessons	Classroom lessons
1 and 2 Use of the dictionary	1. Why do we use the dictionary? How can we locate words quickly in the dictionary? 2. Understanding primary and secondary definitions.	Follow-up to lesson 1: *a.* Noting preferred spellings. *b.* Further practice in locating unfamiliar words. Follow-up to lesson 2: Selecting exact meanings.
3 and 4 Syllabication	1. Listening for parts or syllables as words are pronounced by teacher. 2. Dividing compound words into their parts. 3. Dividing polysyllabic words into syllables.	Follow-up to lesson 1: Further practice in identifying syllables by listening to words. Follow-up to lesson 2: Developing principles of syllabication. Follow-up to lesson 3: Continuing development of principles of syllabication.
5 and 6 Root words	1. Use of root words in recognizing unfamiliar words. 2. Selected prefixes (two or three at a time) introduced.	Follow-up to lesson 1: Further practice in use of root words and study of possibilities of changing meanings of words by adding letters before and after root words. Follow-up to lesson 2: *a.* Selected suffixes (two or three at a time) introduced. *b.* Origin and development

Exhibit III *(Continued)*

Week number and area of study	Large-group lessons	Classroom lessons
		of word meanings; new words that become part of our language; idioms.
7, 8, and 9 Understanding sentences	1. Finding the main idea in a sentence by using key questions. Who did what?	Follow-up to lesson 1: Reinforcement of lesson given in large group, including the finding of the topic sentence and identification of the core of the sentence.
	2. Details of a sentence answer the questions why, where, when, and how.	Follow-up to lesson 2: Details of a sentence; review of question words, why, when, where, and how.
10 and 11 Understanding paragraphs	1. Finding the main idea in a paragraph; selecting the central thought.	Follow-up to lesson 1: Reinforcement of large-group lesson by location of main thought in first sentence in a paragraph and finding the main idea in the last part of the paragraph.
	2. Finding the main idea in a paragraph when it is not stated.	Follow-up to lesson 2: Further practice in inference.
12	1. Review of skills taught in previous eleven weeks.	Follow-up to lesson 1: a. Further review. b. Test administered to determine pupils' progress. c. Pre-testing for selection of pupils who are to be included in the next twelve-week large-group instruction in reading skills. (Pupils whose pre-tests indicate they do not need the next series of lessons may be assigned to another educational area.)

Every large-group lesson should be reviewed in the classroom before the subskill is dealt with. This permits the classroom teacher to determine how much has been learned and what parts of the lesson (if any) need reteaching. This type of evaluation goes on during the entire twelve-week plan (as described above). At the end of this time, a final evaluation is made of tests that have been developed by the teaching team. Students who have done poorly move into smaller groups. For some students, small-group teaching is more effective, just as large-group teaching is more effective for others.

Those who do well on the test are then given a pre-test to determine whether or not they need the next sequence of skills. If, on being pre-tested, some students show high achievement, they are given other subject assignments during the next unit. When the units of work are short, evaluation and regrouping according to needs can take place continuously throughout the school year.

Large-Group Reading Lessons

It is important to remember that some lessons can be effectively presented to large groups and others cannot. For example, a lesson that calls for a great deal of oral participation (such as lessons in phonics and critical reading) may need a small group plan where students have opportunities to speak. Other lessons need not require a large degree of oral participation on the part of the student and can be given effectively to a large group.

A large-group lesson may be given to introduce a skill, with the actual development and application of the skill taking place in the classroom. This however, need not be the only approach; it is possible to follow a large group lesson with another large group lesson in the subskill, a plan recommended if the participating teachers are inexperienced and do not feel competent to create lessons of their own. Then, fewer reading lessons will be given in the classroom and more will be given by the team leader.

Another way to help the inexperienced teacher is to suggest that the classroom lessons be patterned directly after the demonstration lesson. This gives the new teacher practice in presenting well-developed lessons. However, this method is not desirable unless new reading selections and new vocabulary are used within the basic structure.

Each large-group lesson, like a good classroom lesson, should introduce an aim or objective, arouse students' interest, include the actual steps in teaching, summarize, and demonstrate application. A homework assignment may be given if desirable. All homework assignments should be corrected by the participating teacher in the classroom and an analysis of the results presented in the conference with the team leader.

Exhibits IV and V are sample lessons, offered to illustrate the kinds of reading lessons that can be presented to large groups. The materials used in each part of each lesson are listed along the right-hand side of the exhibit. Some lessons will call for specially prepared materials prepared by pupils, participating teachers, and team leader working together. Exhibit VI is an application sheet pertaining to the lesson in Exhibit V.

Materials of Instruction

The master lesson given to a large group may employ a number of teaching aids in addition to those normally used in the classroom. The team leader has time to prepare (or may have the technician prepare) charts, slides, tapes, and films that can be presented attractively to large group classes.

Chalkboards

A chalkboard can be effective only if it can be seen by all students. It is well to note, however, that it is usually difficult to see a chalkboard from a distance of more than thirty feet. Colored chalk such as green or yellow is more easily seen. The writing should be large, well spaced, and legible. Effective use of the chalkboard may be difficult to achieve, however, unless the teacher places the material on the chalkboard before the lesson, for few people have the skill of writing on the chalkboard and still maintaining the attention of the group.

Overhead projectors

The overhead projector is an effective substitute for the chalkboard in teaching large groups. It has a number of advantages:

1. The teacher can face the group at all times.
2. It does not require complete darkness (near-daylight projection).
3. It makes note-taking possible in the room (sufficient light can be allowed).
4. The image is visible to the entire group.
5. Handwriting and illustrations can be projected from the same machine at the same time.
6. Commercially prepared material may be used and, by using overlays, teachers may write or comment without harm to the original.

Exhibit IV

Large-Group Lesson in Word Recognition

Skill:
Learning to look for contextual clues as aids to word recognition and reading.

	Audio-visual materials
Approach (Motivation):	
1. Picture is shown of a detective looking at a "mysterious" object.	Overhead projector, picture flashed on screen.
2. The class is asked if they know what the object is.	
3. One at a time, the teacher adds parts to the picture, showing how the detective finds other objects in the room that help him discover the meaning of the "mysterious" object.	Transparencies placed in succession on original drawing.
4. Group is told that, just as a detective looks for clues to solve a mystery, so we can look for clues to help us recognize words that are "mysterious" to us!	Microphone used by teacher.
Direct teaching techniques:	
1. Teacher presents a difficult word. The meaning should be a "mystery" to most of the group. The teacher offers to help solve the mystery by giving some "word clues."	Word written on acetate and flashed on overhead projector.
2. Sentence is presented that includes the mystery word.	Slide flashed on overhead projector.
3. Volunteers are called on to find the clues.	Words are underlined on acetate projected on screen.
4. Two more sentences presented in similar fashion; students find clue words.	
5. A "Guide for Word Clues" is presented: (*a*) Read the whole sentence. (*b*) Find the word clues. (*c*) What is the meaning of the "mystery word"? (*d*) Read the sentence again to see if it makes sense.	Overhead projector.
6. Students record the "Guide for Word Clues."	Notebooks.
Summary:	
Refer to aim of lesson. Review main steps.	
Follow-up:	
1. Review of contextual-clues lesson.	Use all appropriate visual aids again.
2. Dictionary lesson—checking definition when contextual clues have been used to find a meaning.	

Exhibit V

Large-Group Lesson in Comprehension

	Audio-visual materials

Skill:

Developing the ability to extract the root meaning (main idea) of a sentence by eliminating all details.

Approach (Motivation):

1. Show frame 1 of football player kicking football (simple picture with few details). | Overhead projector.
2. State the idea of this picture, "Jim kicked the football." This tells us *what* is going on in the picture and *who* is doing something. | Use microphone.
3. Remove mask covering caption, "Jim kicked the football," on frame 1. | Overhead projector with overlay removed.

4. Add frame 2 showing grandstands filled with people and labeled "YANKEE STA-DIUM." Frame 2 supplies background to frame 1, and both frames are now seen as one image or overlay. | Overlay frames 1 and 2.

5. Ask individual pupils to point to details on overhead projector. "Who can find a detail in our picture not mentioned in our sentence?" Then ask, "Where did Jim kick the football?"

6. Add the phrase "in crowded Yankee Stadium" to the original sentence, "Jim kicked the football." Remove mask covering this caption on frame 2. | Overlay removed.

7. Flash frame 3 showing floodlights and clock with exact time, 5:45, clearly indicated. This frame should merge with frames 1 and 2 to form a single well-balanced image. | Overhead projector.

8. Repeat step 5 substituting *when* and *where*.

9. Add the phrase "at 5:45 P.M." Remove the mask covering caption on frame 3. The sentence should now read, "Jim kicked the football in crowded Yankee Stadium at 5:45 P.M." Mask the entire picture and raise the projection exposing only the sentence mid-screen.

10. Ask one group to read the complete sentence orally (chorus).

11. State that we have added details to our picture and sentence to get a more complete story, *but* no matter what we add, the *main idea* of our picture and the

79

Exhibit V (*Continued*)

	Audio-visual materials
main idea of our sentence remains the same. "What part of our sentence remained the same?" (Individual response, "Jim kicked the football.")	
12. Reinforce this point by lowering the projection. Remove frame 3 containing the phrase "at 5:45 P.M."	Overhead projector, overlay removed.
13. Have one group chorus what now remains of the sentence.	
14. Remove frame 2 containing the phrase "in crowded Yankee Stadium."	Overlay removed.
15. Repeat step 13.	
16. Remove frame 1 and replace with reading skills page frame. (Aim)	Overlay changed.
17. State the aim of the lesson and expose on overhead projector—How to find the main idea of a sentence by asking questions about the sentence.	
18. Have class read aim silently. Teacher reads orally.	
19. Direct pupils to copy aim onto reading skills page in notebooks.	Notebooks.
20. Ask class to chorus the aim of the lesson.	
21. Flash table of contents page on overhead projector and have class list *finding the main idea of a sentence* on contents page in notebook. Number the skills page.	Overhead projector, new slide.

Direct teaching techniques:

1. Flash a sentence containing details that answer the question *when* and *where* (make sure that the main idea is stated at the beginning of the sentence).	Overhead projector, new slide.
2. Have class read sentence silently while teacher reads orally.	
3. State that we must ask certain questions about the sentence to find main idea, such as *when, where,* etc.	
4. Call upon student to underline words that tell us *when.* Student writes on acetate.	Acetate flashed on overhead projector.
5. Erase underlined phrase.	
6. Call upon student to underline words that tell us *where.*	
7. Repeat step 5.	
8. Ask group to read orally what is left of the sentence.	

80

9. Suggest that what is left is the *main idea*. "We have erased the details that told us when and where. We are left with *what* is going on in the sentence and *who* is doing something."

10. State that *who, what, when* and *where* are not the only questions we might ask in order to find the main idea of a sentence.

11. Repeat step 1 substituting *how* and *why*.

12. Repeat steps 2, 3, 4, 5, 6, 7, and 8, substituting *how* and *why*.

13. Suggest that we now have the *main idea*. "We have erased the details that told us *how* and *why*. We are left with *what* is going on and *who* is doing something."

14. Refer to notebook skills page. Flash, one at a time, the following steps: (*a*) Read the whole sentence. (*b*) Answer the questions *where, when, why, how*. (*c*) Read what is left (main idea). (*d*) Test main idea by asking *who* and *what*.

15. Have group chorus responses to four steps as each is flashed.

16. Application: Distribute application sheets. (*a*) Have group work on finding main ideas and listing details in columns on sheet. (*b*) Check work on overhead projector (individual response).

Application sheet.*
Overhead projector.

Chart.

Summary:
1. Have group chorus aim.
2. Repeat four steps to finding main idea (individual responses).
3. Show chart of huge question mark with words *who, what, when, where, why,* and *how* printed on it.
4. Suggest that class remember to ask these questions whenever they read and that they practice this as they complete today's assignment.

Assignment:
Included on application sheet.

Follow-up:
1. Sentences in which parts of main idea are separated. Example:
In crowded Yankee Stadium, *Jim,* who had been waiting for the signal, *kicked the football.*
2. Sentence in which main idea is found at the end of the sentence.

* See Exhibit VI.

81

Exhibit VI

Application Sheet: Finding the Main Idea of a Sentence

Read the following sentences. Answer the questions *where, when, how,*
and *why.* (Not all the sentences will have the answers to all the questions.)
Fill in your answers in the proper column. Then, *underline* the main idea
of each sentence.

1. Soldiers played football over 2,000 years ago in Greece and Rome
   because they liked the sport.
2. Fifty-four men played the game in Italy as though it were a battle.
3. Indians made footballs out of grass long ago in Mexico.

	WHERE	WHEN	WHY	HOW
1.				
2.				
3.				

For next time:
Practice finding the main idea in these sentences. Follow the steps you used
above. (Remember that not all the sentences will have answers to all the
questions.)

1. Men wear helmets on their heads to protect themselves when they
   play football.
2. Teams practice every day throughout America in order to win their
   games.
3. Football stars are cheered loudly when they score touchdowns if they
   play near their hometowns.

	WHERE	WHEN	WHY	HOW
1.				
2.				
3.				

Exhibit VII

Large-Group Lesson in Studying from Books

	Audio-visual materials

Skill:
Making use of the parts of a book which serve as guides to information contained in the book.

Approach (Motivation):

1. Flash a picture of a man (student) reading; caption states "Send me a man who reads."
2. Question: What does this quotation mean? Students who are widely read generally are able to achieve more. People who read usually increase their knowledge and broaden their interests. Pupils are required to use textbooks for almost all subject areas. Many students do not know how to use a textbook effectively.
3. Today we are going to learn the parts of a book and the use of each part.

Opaque projector.

Direct teaching techniques:
Lesson is taught by means of visual aids illustrating each part of the book. As the visual aid is flashed on the screen the important facts to be remembered will be highlighted. The following visual aids will be used:

a. Cover of the book showing title, author and perhaps an illustration.
b. Title page (title, author, illustrator, publisher, place of publication). Point these out as the features found on the title page. Have a student come to the visual aid, point to each fact mentioned and read aloud.
c. Copyright date (purpose and function); Library of Congress Catalog card numbers.
d. Preface or forward (purpose and function); acknowledgments.
e. Table of contents (divided into main idea and subtopics). Refer to the table of contents students are keeping in their reading notebooks. Have students come to the visual aid and write in new chapter heading under Contents. This one would be *Parts of a Book.*
f. Body of the book (text).
g. Glossary (definition and use).
h. Appendix (mention that every book does not have one).
i. Index (organization and use).

Overhead projector.

Summary:
Question: What information can we learn about each book we read?
Answer: Flash list of the facts learned about the parts of a book. Have the pupils copy them in reading notebooks to keep for future reference and research.

Opaque projector.

Follow-up:
Teacher might want to develop the ability of using the index or perhaps make a comparison between the index and the table of contents.

7. Photocopy machines facilitate the transfer of printed material to overhead visual aids.

Preparing slides and overlays calls for precision and imagination. The school art department can be helpful. Some school systems have technicians whose function it is to prepare slides and overlays. Some of the newer photocopying machines can be used to prepare slides and other visual aids.

These overhead visual aids can be used several times within the same lesson. A teacher may wish to re-project a particular illustration when a concept needs clarification, when a lesson needs summarizing, or when parts of the lesson have to be reviewed before the class can proceed to the next lesson. And, of course, such materials should be shared widely in the school. If the materials are carefully catalogued and made centrally available, circulation of visual aids becomes a simple matter.

Charts

Colorful and carefully lettered charts are effective aids in large-group instruction. They should be elevated for good visibility from every part of the room. An adjustable easel or tripod will provide a comfortable viewing height. A string dropped from a fixture on the ceiling or wall moulding with a large clip at the end is a simple and inexpensive device for chart display. A clothesline strung across the auditorium makes it possible to display charts and pictures by means of removable clips. Charts and pictures can become part of a circulating collection of instructional materials, like the overhead visual aids.

Flannelboards

Flannelboards are particularly useful in large-group instruction because they enable the teacher to place materials in view and to remove them with ease as the lesson develops. Participation by students in the rearrangement of materials on the flannelboard is also possible.

As with charts and pictures, the flannelboard must be placed at a comfortable viewing height.

Tape recorders

Tape recorders serve many purposes for large-group instruction. Sections of lessons may be placed on tape by either students or other members of the team before the actual demonstration. These may take the form of telling a story or reading a poem. The voice of a professional artist reading a scene from a play, a monologue, or an essay may be taped from a phonograph record. During this time the teacher may be putting up materials for the next part of the lesson or spot-correcting students' work sheets. Since a large-group lesson uses primarily a lecture method, a variation of voices is made possible by the introduction of a tape. Tapes are used extensively in the Taylorville Senior High School in Taylorville, Illinois.

As with other specialized instructional materials, these tapes will get maximum use if they are placed in the circulating library.

Duplicated materials

Skill sheets, illustrations, reading selections, and the like, are useful for large-group instruction. Obviously, these materials must be prepared in advance by one of the teaching team members. In large groups that include pupils on several levels of reading ability, duplicated materials serve as a means of differentiating instruction.

Disc recordings

The team leader may cut whole parts of lessons on discs, so that pupils who find they have not mastered the skill or the lesson presented by the teacher may borrow these discs and use them when they meet with the small group or may play them at home.

All instructional materials should be carefully previewed by members of the teaching team. Titles may be misleading; information presented in films may be inaccurate or outdated. Records may be too long to hold the interest of young students. Careful planning is needed to insure proper use of the instructional materials. All instructional materials are supplemental to a lesson and should at no time take the place of the lesson planned by the teaching team. A lesson too dependent upon externally produced instructional materials runs the risk of not encouraging the pupil to participate in the learning process.

Team Orientation for Teachers

Workshops

Optimum success with flexible grouping is most likely to be achieved when it is preceded by in-service orientation for the teaching teams. No matter how capable a teacher may be, the task of instructing three or more classes in one assembly is a formidable one. The teacher may doubt his abilities in this direction and may need guidance. The other members of the team may need direction in the planning of follow-up lessons after the main demonstration or in the techniques of leading small-group discussions. A pre-school-term workshop should provide time to prepare visuals and to obtain appropriate textbooks and practice materials.

Resource persons

Additional help may be obtained by inviting a person from a neighboring school system who has had experience in organizing team teaching. Local universities may recommend faculty members who have acted as consultants in large-group teaching. The film, *And No Bells Ring*, which can be obtained from the NASSP, is an interesting introduction to one of the newer and more creative instructional organizations.

In-service programs for teachers

These should be continued throughout the school year. Instructional patterns change; materials can be improved; groups should be reorganized and teachers made ready to undertake new responsibilities. At the end of the school year, provision should be made to evaluate the program and to plan for the following year. The most successful programs are those that provide for continuous re-evaluation.

Adapting to the School Plant

Of course, the possibilities for flexible grouping in any given school will depend to a large extent on the physical facilities available. Many new school buildings, as well as many old ones, have little or no provision for assembling large groups of students. Probably the closest we have ever come to providing space for teaching more than one class at a time was the old fashioned rolling-door classroom. A school built within the past thirty years usually provides a uniformly limited number of seats in a physically as well as educationally self-contained classroom. Team teaching programs are severely handicapped when forced to function in a typical school building designed with two rows of classrooms of equal size separated by a long narrow corridor. Educational barriers are thus "built-in" in the conventional school building.

Team teaching programs require adjustable areas to accommodate groups of various sizes—from 150 students to one or two students studying by themselves. Regrouping into units of different sizes is frequently necessary and should be facilitated. However, each group of children should always be assigned a homeroom class to which it reports at the beginning and the end of each school day. Space should also be provided for teachers to meet and work privately, and there should be a workroom for the preparation of special instructional materials.

In some systems, the trend is toward installing movable partitions in school buildings, whereby several classroom areas may be combined. Smaller units are built for discussion groups and individual study areas are built around the central library.

In Englewood, Florida, a school building has been designed to provide four different kinds of educational space. There are four conventional classrooms averaging 1,000 square feet each; one "super classroom" of 1,500 square feet that can be divided into two small classrooms of 750 square feet each by means of a vinyl accordian partition; and a double classroom of 2,000 square feet, also divisible by partition into two regular classrooms of 1,000 square feet each.

These classrooms of diverse size are exploited fully to raise the level of instruction in the following fashion: Teachers of six- and seven-year-olds and teachers of seven- and eight-year-olds merge their classes for part of the school day. These two groups are assigned to one of the larger classrooms. By planning as a team throughout the year, the teachers are able to cut across class and grade lines in order to group children according to their educational needs rather than their chronological age. For example, all children capable of reading on a fourth-grade level are grouped together for reading instruction even though some of them may be in the first and second grades. Children who need beginning reading, whether first or fourth graders, are grouped for instruction on a beginner's level. This instructional flexibility is possible largely because of the adaptability of the space at the disposal of the teachers.

Carson City, Michigan, has a new elementary school consisting of three separate areas of open spaces, each area the equivalent of four conventional classrooms. Two areas are for academic purposes and the third for administrative offices, teachers' lounges, kitchens, multipurpose rooms, and health education areas. In this school, there are no individual classrooms; the teachers decide cooperatively how the free space is to be apportioned. Every three weeks the teachers in each area meet to plan the program and allocate space for the next three-week period. When school starts each morning, the children go to their home areas to which they are assigned. There are no permanent desks; all furniture is completely movable. Throughout the day, children and furniture move quickly within a large unencumbered space. Groups change in composition and size as the teaching program requires.

New schools designed to provide for instructional flexibility are being constructed in a number of cities in different parts of the country. The Educational Facilities Laboratories [3] publishes profiles of schools that have been designed for flexible educational programs. (See Suggested Reading at end of chapter: "Schools in the Program.")

Getting the most out of available space

The maximum use of space in our existing plants should be of major concern to teachers and supervisors. Restrictions imposed by the physical plant should not be allowed to discourage new approaches in team teaching. In every school there are some large areas, such as gymnasiums, auditoriums, lunchrooms, or multipurpose rooms, which can be used to assemble large groups of children. In adapting any of these areas for large groups, the following suggestions might be considered:

Desk room. The seats in the lunchroom often have arms that can be used for writing surfaces. If not, the lunchroom table can be used for that purpose. For auditorium seats, lap boards are recommended. In the gymnasium or the multipurpose room, folding chairs, which can be stored, may be used with lap boards. In both these rooms raised platforms for teachers may be necessary, because all the seats will be on the same level.

Dark shades. Slides and films are often used for large-group instruction, and when they are, it may be necessary to reduce lighting for effective projection on screens.

Electrical outlets. Many outlets are necessary to accommodate audio-visual aids that are used in large-group instruction. Overloading of electrical circuits should be avoided, and there should be enough power to run several machines at the same time. Providing more electrical outlets is well worth the cost.

Ventilation. Fans and exhausts can be provided to aid proper circulation of air in the large group instruction area. Many of the older buildings were constructed without considering the adequacy of the

[3] Educational Facilities Laboratories, Inc., 477 Madison Avenue, New York 22, N. Y.

ventilation. It is important, therefore, to investigate means of increasing the air circulation in such areas.

Acoustics. Attention should always be given to the problem of acoustics. A lunchroom may very well have acoustical tiles on the ceiling, whereas a gymnasium may have been built without consideration of noise control. If, during a lesson, a teacher notices that a group of students has lost interest or is not paying attention, she may investigate the possibility of a "dead spot." The teacher's first step would be to move this group to another area in the room and, if possible, a sound engineer should be called in to recommend corrective procedures.

Provision must be made for the comfort of *small groups* as well as large ones. A classroom with movable furniture, for example, permits the small group to gather in one section of the room for informal discussion. Individual students may meet with teachers in the library, in lounges, or in offices.

Films, Filmstrips, and Slides in Flexible Grouping

Films, filmstrips, and slides can enrich and extend learning experiences. Beyond that, they allow students to work in large groups, clusters, or independently, depending upon specific needs. The teacher can use these flexible media to present a lesson or to implement parts of lessons.

Films have advantages similar to large-group teaching, since a lesson given by an expert can be viewed on film by many more students than would be possible in a conventionally sized classroom. In fact, a film, which can be used again and again, can reach even more students than can a master teacher in an auditorium. Films, like textbooks, should be reviewed and previewed before they are used. The purpose for which they are used should be clearly defined and the student audience carefully selected, so that only students who can benefit from the content and the film medium will see it.

Large groups of students can be assembled in an auditorium or school theatre to view a film. Viewing conditions should be good and sound clear and audible. A film may present an actual lesson or it may present some phase of the subject used to enrich or implement the curriculum. In the program conducted by the State of Utah, nine high schools use films to teach physics, and twelve junior high schools use slides and tapes for giving vocational information.

Since the classroom teacher is not involved in the presentation, it is important that follow-up lessons be planned as in large group instruction.

Films have many advantages. They can sometimes be in color, and they are animated. Sound films, with the simultaneous presentation of auditory and visual impressions, are effective in teaching reading. However, the film, like the telecast, proceeds at its own pace without control by the teacher. And if the pace is not right for the group, the teacher must be prepared to take over.

Films and filmstrips can be used by conventionally sized groups as well as small groups and individual students. Filmstrips are used in the New Castle, Pennsylvania, reading experiment. The content of the filmstrip closely parallels the material covered in a companion basal reader series. The initial reading instruction for each new lesson is presented on the screen. The reader is used after the screen presentation.

However, this approach, as it is used in New Castle, requires that all children use the same reader as well as the same filmstrip. When either is inappropriate for the group or for individual readers, progress in reading is adversely affected.

Filmstrips can be used for small groups. Students who are having difficulty with particular reading skills can meet in pairs to look at and listen to specially prepared films. Filmstrips have a number of other advantages. The teacher or pupils can control the speed and pace it to the needs of the pupils. The filmstrip usually has both depth and color and can be useful for specific training in such reading skills as word recognition, comprehension, and vocabulary study. However, the strip film does have a set sequence. In this respect slides have greater flexibility.

The following is a partial listing of films and filmstrips, in the area of reading, that are currently available:

Films (16mm)

Build Your Vocabulary. Coronet Films, Coronet Building, Chicago, Ill.
Dramatizes the need for self-improvement in vocabulary.
Discovering the Library. Coronet Films, Coronet Building, Chicago, Ill.
Introduces children to the public library.
Do Words Ever Fool You? Coronet Films, Coronet Building, Chicago, Ill.
The importance of careful use and interpretation of words is presented in a simple form, a drama.
How to Read a Book. Coronet Films, Coronet Building, Chicago, Ill.
The intelligent use of the various parts of a book.

It's All Yours. Teen Age Book Club, 251 Fourth Avenue, New York 10, N. Y.
Emphasizes value of reading as an avenue to adventure in life.

It's Your Library. Mahnke Productions, 215 East Third Street, Des Moines 9, Iowa.
Explains essentials of a library and how pupils may use it profitably.

Let's Read Poetry. Bailey Films, 2044 North Berendo Street, Hollywood 27, Calif.
Suggestions for improving oral reading of poetry.

Look It Up! Coronet Films, Coronet Building, Chicago, Ill.
Designed to promote better dictionary habits and wider use of the dictionary.

Maps and Their Uses. Coronet Films, Coronet Building, Chicago, Ill.
Teaches reading of symbols, grids, legends and other map characteristics.

Maps Are Fun. Coronet Films, Coronet Building, Chicago, Ill.
Dramatization of map making.

Poems Are Fun. Coronet Films, Coronet Building, Chicago, Ill.
Promotes enjoyment in reading and writing poems and in choral speaking.

We Discover the Dictionary. Coronet Films, Coronet Building, Chicago, Ill.
Training in use of the dictionary for meaning, spelling, and pronunciation.

What Is a Map? Young America Films, 18 East 41 Street, New York 17, N. Y.
Animation and description of simple maps of home and community.

Who Makes Words? Coronet Films, Coronet Building, Chicago, Ill.
The growth and change in meanings of words.

Filmstrips

Filmstrips on Phonics: "Vowel Sounds Help You"; "Your Eyes and Ears Are Good Helpers"; "Test Yourself on Sounds"; "The Vowel is the Backbone of a Syllable." Society for Visual Education, 1545 Diversey Parkway, Chicago 14, Ill.

How to Read: to Understand, to Evaluate, to Use. Society for Visual Education, 1545 Diversey Parkway, Chicago 14, Ill.
Designed to promote better use and interpretation of books using cartoons.

How to Use an Encyclopedia. Popular Science, Audio-Visual Division, 354 Fourth Avenue, New York, N. Y.
Using the encyclopedia in the classroom.

Library Series. Young America Films, 18 East 14 Street, New York 17, N. Y.
Six strips on the dictionary, encyclopedia, Dewey decimal system, card catalog, etc.

Your Dictionary and How To Use It. Society for Visual Education, 1545 Diversey Parkway, Chicago 14, Ill.
Instruction in the use of a dictionary.

Television in Flexible Grouping

Television can be used for reading instruction in much the same way as films or filmstrips. Students can be grouped in large units and small units to view telecasts. As with master teachers and films, television can bring high quality teaching to large groups of students. The evaluations of television instruction in reading seem to show that it is at least as effective as conventional methods, and more effective for lower aptitude groups.[4]

Teaching reading by television, however, presents several problems. Words, sentences, paragraphs, and selections must be presented so as to take into account the limited image area of the television screen. This means that, with present equipment, only a few words will fit on a line and only short selections are feasible. Long passages not only consume valuable time; they seriously reduce pupil interest. There is also the problem of pacing lessons to suit all pupils. The classroom teacher has no control; the lesson proceeds regardless of the reaction of the students. Students learn at varying rates and the television teacher is unable to be guided by an "unseen" audience.

As with all audio-visual media, it is important to create proper conditions for optimum viewing in the classroom. The New York State Department of Education makes the following suggestions:

Utilize a 21- or 24-inch receiver with front mounted speaker if possible.
Face receiver away from window wall at an angle of 35 to 45 degrees to eliminate reflections.
Place receiver high enough to be seen with ease.
Some schools employ metal stands with rubber casters.
Seat pupils at reasonable distance from the receiver.
Eye fatigue decreases attention and develops rapidly in children.
Seat pupils with defective hearing or vision in accordance with their needs.
View programs in normal light. Do not darken room.
Adjust sound for comfortable listening.
Adjust picture for proper brightness and contrast.[5]

Experiments in television teaching

Working with the Board of Education of New York City, the New York State Board of Regents supported a reading television series for

[4] William H. Allen, "Audio Visual Materials," *Review of Educational Research,* XXVI (April 1956), pp. 125–126.
[5] *Regents Educational Television Project 1959–1960,* Albany: New York State Education Department, 1959, p. 4.

two years. The main objective of this series was to teach the basic reading skills.

The series was divided into two tracks, one of which gave remedial help, while the other taught developmental reading skills. Students for the telecasts, were grouped according to their reading needs. For some lessons, two whole classes were combined; other lessons were watched by only those students who needed a particular skill. Some teachers used the television lessons in the regular classroom as part of the course of study. It would be impossible to report in this chapter all the variations in group patterns that were employed by the schools.

Under the direction of the present author, who was the reading supervisor, two reading consultants worked on the scope and sequence to be taught through television. A "Teachers' Guide" was developed as an aid in preparing for the television lesson and as a resource bulletin for follow-up instruction. This publication enabled the classroom teachers to prepare their classes for the telecast, to direct the students' viewing, and to reinforce the telecasts with meaningful follow-up lessons.

The television lessons were not designed to duplicate a classroom situation. Emphasis was placed on charts, pictures, graphs, and printed materials which were unusual, vivid and especially suitable to the medium of television. These materials were designed to take maximum advantage of television instruction, but were also readily adaptable to classroom use. The result of the program was that large numbers of students received expert instruction through the efforts of a handful of reading specialists. The television lessons, by letting one actually see the implementation of the suggestions in the "Teachers' Guide," proved to be a stimulating training device for teachers viewing the programs in their classrooms. All the telecasts were put on film (kinescopes) and became the basis for in-service courses in the teaching of reading for teachers.

Evaluation of this series showed that students viewing the telecasts gained slightly in reading achievement over students who did not view the series. However, it could not be clearly determined whether or not the telecasts were the cause of this improvement. It is more likely that the stimulation of being involved in an experiment might have been one cause for the improvement and the training aspect for the teacher may have been another cause of improved instruction. Exhibits VIII and IX show two sample lesson plans from this series, including pre-telecast suggestions, the telecast content, the post-telecast suggestions for follow-up.

Exhibit VIII

Teachers' Guide for Television Lessons—the Corrective Series

Topic: "Kingpin of Ideas," Developing the ability to find the main idea in a paragraph.

Objectives: Developing the following abilities and understandings:
1. Finding the main thought in a paragraph where the main idea is stated in the first sentence.
2. Finding the main thought in a paragraph where the main idea is stated in the last sentence.
3. Finding the main thought in a paragraph where the main idea is stated in the body of the paragraph.
4. Finding the main thought in a paragraph where the main idea is not stated but implied.

Pre-telecast suggestions for the classroom teacher: Conduct these activities:
1. Finding the main idea in a complex sentence. Example:
      "He came to the party despite the rain."
2. Finding the main idea in a wordy, complicated sentence. Example:
      "As soon as his mother's back was turned, the dirty-faced little boy ate the delicious, creamy, chocolate cake in the kitchen as if he had never eaten cake before."
3. Developing a chart showing how the guide words: where, when, how, why and words of description, can reduce the sentence to its main idea. Example:
4. Applying grammar to these key words from the sentence.
                "Boy"   "ate"   "cake"
                 subject   verb   object
5. Applying grammar to the guide words and words of description. Example:
                Adverbial phrase, adjectives, etc.
6. Providing practice for reducing complicated sentences of all curriculum areas to the key words which comprise the main thought. Example:
      "When he was a little boy living in Mount Vernon, Washington chopped down the beautiful cherry tree his father prized so greatly."
      Using the guide words, pupils erase those words which answer where, when, how, why, and all words of description.

Exhibit VIII (*Continued*)

7. Given only key words, pupils use guide words to add adverbial phrases and adjectives to build sentences.

Telecast content:
1. *In the introduction,* a visual approach highlights the fact that a reading selection will always have a central theme, that it may contain minor related ideas affecting the central theme and fusing with it to form a single unified whole.
2. *In the direct teaching,* these techniques are used:
   a. A pupil participation activity is used to direct pupils how to choose the most appropriate heading for the selection from given multiple-choice lists.
   b. Students are then shown how to find the main idea when it is stated somewhere within the paragraph.
   c. Other paragraphs are analyzed to note the main idea when it is not stated in the paragraph but it is implied.
   d. During the course of the preceding activities, a chart is developed: (1) as an aid to the pupils in the lesson and (2) as a future resource.
   e. The lesson is summarized in a review of the uses of the skill taught.
3. *In the conclusion,* the skill of the day is noted on the skills chart and other reading skills used in the lesson are identified.

Post-telecast suggestions for the classroom teacher:
1. Afford more practice in finding the main idea in paragraphs in which the main idea is not stated but implied.
2. Use a newspaper to reinforce the value of headings and lead paragraphs in articles.
3. Show value of appropriate titles and main ideas as aids in organizing thoughts for writing compositions.
4. Develop understanding that other details of a paragraph explain or support the main idea.

Additional resource (Teacher resource):
Harris, Albert, *How to Increase Reading Ability* (3rd ed.), Longmans, Green, New York, 1956.

Exhibit IX

Teachers' Guide for Television Lessons—Developmental Series

Topic: "Success Assured," developing the ability to follow printed directions.

Objectives: Developing the following abilities and understandings:
1. Interpreting and following printed directions.
2. Recognizing the need for *one* careful preliminary reading to get a general understanding of the directions as a whole.
3. Recognizing the need for *rereading* to get a clear understanding of the purpose of each step in its sequential order.
4. Visualizing the steps in the directions for a clearer understanding of the quantities, objects needed, measurements, etc.

Pre-telecast suggestions for classroom teacher:
1. Read the parts of the science textbook which explain how to perform experiments.
2. Practice describing how to hit a ball, how to run a boat, etc.
3. In preparation for a classroom bulletin board display, have pupils bring in labels from cans, boxes, etc. which give directions on how to use their contents.

Telecast content:
1. *In the introduction,* the teacher develops the purpose of the telecast by using visual materials that illustrate some humorous and serious results of failing to follow directions.
2. *In the direct teaching,* the teacher uses the following techniques to develop the lesson:
    a. Several different types of printed directions are read: (1) a science experiment, (2) a cooking recipe, (3) how to make a specific item, and (4) how to play a specific game.
    b. Certain similarities are pointed out in each set: (1) a specifically stated purpose, (2) specifically stated measurements, objects, materials, etc., and (3) specifically stated steps in sequential order.
    c. One specific experiment in science is read and its purpose, its *measurements, objects* and *materials,* and its steps are listed.
    d. The possible result of the experiment is discussed. The experiment would result in failure if: any incorrect materials were to be used; the steps were to be performed out of their sequential order; or any steps were to be left out altogether.

Exhibit IX (*Continued*)

e. A chart, "Following Directions," is examined. Step 1: Read the directions *once* for a general understanding of the steps to be followed. Step 2: Reread the directions to understand the measurements, and the objects and the materials needed in the experiments, *and* to visualize each step in its sequential order.

f. The steps on the chart are applied to a specific cooking recipe, the pupils participating in this application under the direction of the teacher.

g. A self-checking device is given so pupils can check their work in their notebooks.

h. The skill of the day is underlined on the "Reading Skills Chart" on the bulletin board.

i. The specific careers that require the ability to use this reading skill are checked on the career chart.

3. *In the conclusion,* the teacher summarizes the outcomes of the lesson:

a. Interpreting and following printed directions is an essential part of every day life.

b. The ability to follow printed directions is a skill learned in school.

c. Success in following directions is assured if the directions are read carefully, the details carried out in sequential order, and the terms understood.

Post-telecast suggestions for the classroom teacher:

1. Prepare a colorful bulletin board display with "Following Directions" as its theme, using the labels from cans, boxes, etc., which the pupils have brought to class. Include in the display some cooking recipes found in magazines and newspapers brought to class by the pupils.

2. Have the pupils actually prepare a specific food as explained in a cooking recipe.

3. Have the pupils bring to class their own sets of directions for making a toy, a boat, or other article to determine if the directions can be followed to a successful conclusion by their classmates.

Additional resource (Teacher resource):

Reading: Grades 7, 8, and 9, Bureau of Publications, Board of Education, New York, 1960.

The Cortland television experiment

Since 1959, the Cortland elementary schools have been participating in a closed-circuit television series. Fourth, fifth, and sixth grade students receive reading lessons on television three times a week. Word analysis, vocabulary, comprehension, library skills, and literature appreciation were emphasized. The lessons are aimed at the average group at each grade level and each classroom teacher has a complete lesson outline. Class groups remain in their own classrooms; no attempt is made to combine groups. A variety of commercial and especially prepared materials has been used for the television lessons.

The results of the experiment showed that the students reactions were favorable for the most part. However, as with most mass media, it was found that superior readers made significantly smaller gains following television instruction than in previous years. The below-average readers gained significantly more than in the previous year in which there was no television teaching. The average readers made normal gains. It could then be concluded that the whole-class approach to teaching reading, whether by the teacher, a film or a telecast, benefits some pupils and is detrimental to others.

The Dade County experiment

A telecourse in reading improvement is being offered by the Reading Clinic and the Dade County Junior College in Miami, Florida. It is on open circuit, so students may view the telecasts at home and then meet in small groups for further instruction. The program consists of thirty-six telecasts presented twice weekly. The programs cover the following skills: speed of perception and reading rate; vocabulary development; paragraph and sentence comprehension; intensive reading; and others.

The students receive study guides, workbooks, and textbooks to supplement the series. When the students meet in small groups, instructors handle the checking of assignments, student questions, group meetings and conferences, and special testing periods.

On the basis of available test data, there are no appreciable differences in reading performance between students attending actual reading classes and those who work at home with instruction through television.

The Hagerstown experiment

Two reading programs, a Reading Skills Program and a Controlled Reader Program, are offered in the Washington County Closed-Circuit

Educational Television Project in Maryland. Eight thousand pupils participate in the project in grades one through six in twenty-nine television-connected schools. One studio teacher can reach approximately 350 classrooms in the elementary schools.

Selection of participants is a matter for the classroom teacher to decide. An entire class may participate as a group or selected pupils may form one or more groups in a given classroom or join similar groups. Some pupils enter at the beginning, others at midyear and still others near the end of the school year. Pupils are encouraged to stay in the program for as long as the offering meets their needs, interests, and abilities. The classroom teacher guides the pupils in follow-up activities and appraises individual lessons in order to keep the studio teacher aware of the reactions of these students.

Data currently available suggest that pupils in the program seem to be motivated to apply the skills learned, and teachers favor the continuation of the program. These "findings," however, are based on opinion and sample evidence and an intensive evaluation is presently in process.

Language Laboratories in Flexible Grouping

Language laboratories were introduced primarily in the teaching of foreign languages, but they are now finding new uses in connection with flexible grouping. For example, teachers in Redwood City, California, are experimenting with this device in teaching first graders to read. Special lightweight headsets permit 6-year-olds to listen to recorded sounds of English vowels, consonants, and combination sounds. While the children are listening to the sounds, they see a picture of the word, the letters that form it, and the position of the lips in creating the sound. These pictures are in an accompanying book.

This system was developed by Dr. Helen Burke, director of the reading clinic in Palo Alto, California. In an evaluation of this approach, first graders were found to have high levels of achievement in reading, writing, spelling, and language.

The language laboratory appears to have added an important dimension to reading programs. Because the tapes used are inexpensive to prepare, reading instruction can be tailored to needs of specific individuals. Therefore, when some students are meeting in large groups, others can be using a language laboratory. Although the use of language laboratories for reading instruction is still in the developmental stage, the future of these devices looks bright.

Self-Selection (Individualized Reading) for Flexible Grouping

The term "self-selection" has a more appropriate connotation than the commonly used term, "individualized reading," since all reading is individual. The program offers the opportunity for the student to select his own reading material. Basal readers are eliminated as the core of reading instruction since they impose a uniform reading selection. In the self-selection program, students have access to many more books in keeping with their interests and reading abilities.

Under the teacher's guidance, the student selects the book he wishes to read from a large variety of books. Periods are set aside for the student to read quietly and independently. During these periods students are assigned an individual conference time with the teacher. At these conferences, the teacher and the student discuss his reading, and specific skills are taught as needed. The teacher often uses a checklist to record skills taught, books read, and progress noted. The stigma of being placed in a "low group" is removed as each student functions independently on his own level and "reading groups," as such, are usually not employed.

Even though the individual conference is an important component in the self selection program it is not its sole feature. Periods are set aside when pupils meet as a class, for sharing and evaluating books they have read. The self-selection program offers high motivation because of the number and variety of books available to the student. It also fulfills the universal desire to have a time "of his own" with the teacher. There is much to commend this approach, and articles and books by Miel[6] and Veatch[7] describe the self-selection program in detail. The self-selection approach places great demands on the teacher and should, therefore, be tried only by well-prepared teachers. Also, it is recommended that this approach not be introduced before adequate reading materials are available. Crucial to the success of this program is a large quantity of circulating books. There should be a minimum of ten trade books per child, suited, of course, to his reading and interest levels. In addition to trade books, magazines, newspapers, and dictionaries, there should be available copies of appropriate text books in all curriculum areas so that the teacher may use these when developing special reading skills.

[6] Alice Miel, Ed., *Individualized Reading Practices*, New York: Bureau of Publications, Teachers College, Columbia University, 1958.

[7] Jeannette Veatch, Ed., *Individualized Reading*, New York: Putnam, 1959.

The self-selection program does, however, raise a number of questions as to its effectiveness for universal use in schools. Can every teacher with thirty students in a class have sufficient time for individual conferences in order to provide for careful evaluation and instruction in the conference? Can a teacher realistically keep detailed records for each student which would allow for teaching systematic sequence of reading skills? How much reading is done by the slow learner who cannot read fluently and therefore cannot read extensively? Can every classroom be provided with an abundant supply of books within the interest and ability ranges of the students? Are most teachers sufficiently familiar with children's literature to be able to help them in selecting books?

So far, research has told us little about the effectiveness of this program. Most of the research has been too limited in scope and too uncontrolled to prove anything conclusively.

Evaluation of the Program

A program should be evaluated and its accomplishments measured in terms of the purposes for which it was established. We want to know not only if pupils are acquiring the basic knowledge requirements, but also if they are applying these skills to independent study. Students should be tested when they enter a program, periodically throughout the school year, and upon completion of the term's work. Ruth Strang lists some general procedures for evaluation: [8]

1. Evaluation should be continuous rather than periodic.

2. It should be a part of the instructional program, not apart from it.

3. It should obtain evidence as to the extent to which the stated objectives have been achieved.

4. In obtaining this evidence, it should use both formal and informal methods.

5. The data collected should be used for the improvement of programs and procedures.

6. Increasing emphasis should be placed on self-appraisal as the student grows older.

7. Evaluation of a reading program should be carried on by a team that includes administrators, reading consultants, other specialists, teachers, students, and parents.

[8] Ruth Strang, "Development In And Through Reading," *National Society for the Study of Education Yearbook*, University of Chicago Press, Chicago, Ill., 1961, pp. 381–382.

Standardized tests

Since most school systems use standardized tests to measure achievement, students in flexible-group teaching situations should be included in the total school general testing program. The question is, does the achievement of individual students in the large and small groups fall behind, equal, or excel the achievement of students with equal ability who are taught in a more conventional class? However, administrators and teachers should be cautious in evaluating programs, teachers, or students on the basis of standardized test results. A number of variables —teacher differences, composition of student groups, test awareness, etc.—must be considered in evaluating the effectiveness of a program.

Informal (teacher-made) tests

These tests can offer a teacher a day-by-day measure of students' progress. Approaches can be changed, content altered, and individual students given reinforcement experiences by a constant informal type of evaluation.

Informal tests may take many forms. Students can be asked to evaluate their own reading growth. Short selections may be given to the student to read that can indicate to a teacher the student's reading ability and give some clues as to his disabilities. Some publishers provide informal tests with their basal reading series.

The results of using informal reading inventories can be used with full effectiveness *only* when:

1. the teachers are aware of the purposes of the testing program and accept them as part of the instructional program;
2. the students recognize that the tests can be used for self analysis and guidance and not as a threat or rating device;
3. the parents understand the purposes and uses of tests in the school's instructional program;
4. the school administration recognizes that the primary purpose of testing is the improvement of instruction and not administrative decision making. Tests used as administrative whips lose their effectiveness as instructional tools.

Student and faculty reactions

When a school is being reorganized for flexible grouping, it is not only important to gather evidence on the progress of the students, it is equally important to know the reaction of supervisors and teachers to a new organization.

The principal, supervisors and teachers might be interested in the answers to the following questions:

1. Does this type of learning experience enrich the instructional program of the school?
2. Is there evidence of deeper insights, more positive attitudes, and effective learning on the part of the students?
3. Are the teachers becoming more skillful in their new roles?
4. Does the program work toward the better deployment of the professional personnel?
5. How can this program be improved?
6. Should it be retained, extended, or limited?

Students, on the other hand, evaluate a program in other ways. Are they more interested in the subject matter because of this new type of grouping? Are they achieving as well—or better—or less than they have been in the established conventional organization?

A few questions that could be asked of students at the end of a semester might be in the following form:

	More	*The same*	*Less*
1. Do you find this new type of grouping is as interesting as the regular classroom lessons?	____	_____	____
2. Do you think you are able to learn as much as you can in a regular classroom?	____	_____	____
3. Do you find it as easy to follow and understand (large group, television, film, language lab) lessons as a regular classroom lesson?	____	_____	____
4. Do you find that regrouping in small units for special work is as helpful as grouping in the regular classroom?	____	_____	____

5. What suggestions can you offer to improve this new organization? Be specific as to time spent in instruction, materials used and mechanical equipment.

An evaluation of any given organization will always require that a combination of methods be used; standardized tests, informal measures, observation, professional and student reactions. The purpose of evaluation is to improve a program; therefore it should be closely connected with instruction and the students personal development.

Today there is a marked interest in new organizations, but it should be kept in mind that an organization is but a means to an end. Extensive experimentation and research are needed to evaluate different types of flexible grouping before a school adopts a new pattern for organization. It is for the professional staff of a school to decide which group pattern or combination of patterns produces the most effective learning.

Suggested Reading

Aaron, Ira E., Frances Goodwin, and Vada Kent, "Fourth Grade Teachers Experiment with Cross-Class Grouping for Reading Instruction," *Elementary English*, 36 (May 1959), pp. 305–307.

An Administrator Guide to Reading Educational Leadership, Series Z, Department of Public Instruction, Harrisburg, Pa., 1958.

Bogdan, Amela, "The Work of Reading Counselors," *Reading for Today's Children*, National Elementary Principal, 35, No. 1 (September 1955), pp. 202–206.

Controversial Issues in the Classroom, National Education Association, Washington, D. C., 1961.

de Bernarde, Arno, Victor Doherty, Evrett Hummel, and Charles William Buebaker, *Planning Schools for New Media*, Department of Health, Education and Welfare, Government Printing Office, Washington, D. C., 1961.

Goodlad, John I., and Robert H. Anderson, *The Nongraded Elementary School*, Harcourt Brace, New York, 1959.

Local School Construction Programs, Department of Health, Education and Welfare, Government Printing Office, Washington, D. C., 1957.

Planning, Designing the Multi-Purpose Room in Elementary School, Department of Health, Education and Welfare, Government Printing Office, Washington, D. C., 1954.

Planning for Schools with Television, Education Facilities Laboratories, Ford Foundation for the Advancement of Education, New York, 1960.

Policies to Help Guide Boards of Education, School Administrators, Classroom Teachers, National Education Association, Washington, D. C., 1961.

Ross, Donald H. (Ed.), *Administration for Adaptability*, New York Metropolitan School Study Committee, New York, 1958.

The Secondary School Plant—An Approach for Functional Facilities, Department of Health, Education and Welfare, Government Printing Office, Washington, D. C., 1956.

Trump, J. Lloyd, *New Horizons for Secondary School Teachers*, Ford Foundation for the Advancement of Education, New York, 1961.

————, *Images of the Future—A New Approach to the Secondary School*, National Association of Secondary School Principals, Washington, D. C., 1959.

————, and Dorsey Baynham, *Focus on Change—Guide to Better Schools*, Rand McNally, Chicago, 1961.

4 Programed Materials in Reading Instruction

The "programing" of instruction, as the term is here used, is not a new approach to teaching. The research of Pavlov, Poe, Spence, and others has demonstrated that when a stimulus-response-reward pattern is repeated often enough, learning takes place. Pigeons, for example, have learned highly involved patterns of behavior (pecking a specific number of times on different colored buttons to receive food) by application of this psychological principle. The results of these animal learning studies were formalized by experimental psychologists and applied to human learning.

In programing, each step is broken down into discrete bits of information. The student reads an instruction, a question, or an incompleted sequence; he then answers or responds by filling in a blank; he checks his answer to see if it is correct and then moves on to the next step. Each question or item is called a *"frame."* Each answer is called a *"response."* Programers have given the name *"cuing"* to the technique that is used to insure a correct response. A cue is a subtle hint which suggests the correct answer. There are different types of cuing, the limit depending on a programer's ingenuity. When a response is being introduced, a programer maximizes the number of cues. We know that a student knows his subject when he responds correctly without any cues. Cues are withdrawn gradually; the term for withdrawing cues is *"fading."*

To insure that the student has really learned what has been taught, the terminal behavior should be repeated several times at intervals in the program. A good program reviews and tests as it proceeds.

105

The Constructed Response (Linear Programing)

B. F. Skinner of Harvard, using this technique, developed a teaching approach which presents as its basis a meticulously structured series of questions or items arranged so that each item leads (cues) the student into making the correct response. Each item or step, carefully organized in logical sequence, requires a response from the student. Before he proceeds to the next step or item, the students is shown the correct response and he checks this against his answer. Since each successive item and correct response is based on the preceding item and correct reponse, the program provides for continuing positive reinforcement. The student, by giving the maximum number of correct answers, is led into a terminal behavior which is the object of the lesson. The problem for the programer—and it is a complex one—is to evolve a detailed sequence of small steps which will lead the student to the desired outcome with a minimum of errors along the way.

A Programed Primer on Programing [1] describes in program form the principles of programing. While it repeats some of what has been said above, it is presented, in Exhibit I, as both a simple and concise statement of the procedures involved and to show what it is like to do a program.

Confirm your answer (response) before proceeding to the next item (frame). The answer to each item can be found in the box on the left side of the page parallel with the next question.

[1] *A Programed Primer on Programing*, Center for Programed Instruction, New York, 1960, pp. 2–23.

Exhibit I

A Programed Lesson in Programing

	1. Teaching is the arranging of conditions that enable a student to learn. *Programed instruction* is a new technique of arranging the conditions of learning, so p_____d instruction is a teaching technique.
1. programed	2. *Instructional techniques,* such as lectures, discussions, and audio-visual aids, can implement differing educational philosophies or goals. The new technique of programed i_____ can likewise implement _____ educational philosophies.
2. instruction differing(ent)	3. Many philosophies of education can be implemented by the new technique of teaching called _____ _____.
3. programed instruction	4. Programed instruction is a teaching _____; it (is, is not) a philosophy of education.

4. technique (or method) is not	5. Programed instruction brings into the classroom *effective and efficient* techniques developed by experimental psychologist for teaching complex behavior. Learning probably occurs under many diverse conditions, but programed instruction employs those conditions found to be most _____ and _____.
5. effective (and) efficient (Either order will do.)	6. One condition which has been shown to facilitate learning is called *"reinforcement."* Programed instruction employs techniques that facilitate learning. You might expect that programed instruction uses "_____" to facilitate learning.
6. reinforcement	7. In ordinary English, "reinforce" is a synonym of "strengthen." Something that strengthens behavior can be said, then, to "_____" the behavior.
7. reinforce	8. To psychologists, behavior which is likely to occur, i.e. is very probable, is "strong." (The behavior doesn't have to be noisy or forceful!) When a particular bit of behavior, a response, is strengthened by reinforcement the response is more _____ than it was before being reinforced.
8. likely (to occur) or probable	9. Some consequences, i.e., events which *follow* a response, increase the likelihood of a repetition of the response. If the consequence makes the response more likely, psychologists say it "r_____s" the behavior.

reinforces	10. A response is reinforced by something which comes _____ the response occurs.
after	11. To psychologists, reinforcement is a "class of events" which comes _____ the response and which can be shown to make the response _____ to recur.
after more likely or likely	12. Anyone who has taught tricks to his dog knows how to use reinforcement. In teaching the dog to "speak," he waits for the bark that follows the command "Speak!" As soon as the dog barks, the master gives it _____ (in your own words).
dog candy, a piece of food, a pat on the head, etc. or a reinforce-ment	13. When a student correctly answers a question in class, the teacher is likely to say, "Right." When a student correctly answers most of the questions on a test, he may be given an A. "Right" and A's are examples of _____ that can be used in the classroom.
reinforce-ment (or reinforcing events, or reinforcers)	14. Although there is (usually) only one "correct" spelling of a word, students have many ways of "spelling" words which teachers somehow manage to decipher. If we want the correct spelling to occur whenever the student writes a particular word, we should arrange for some kind of r_____ to follow the correct response.

109

14. reinforce- ment	15. When an animal is trained in the laboratory, the ex- perimenter may reinforce the "correct" response by giving food to the hungry animal *immediately* after the response is made. When a child or adult participates in a learning experiment, the experimenter may say "Right" *immediately* after the correct response is made. Saying "Right!" usually provides r_____ment for the human learner.
15. reinforce- ment	16. Psychologists, educators, and others who have done research in the training of complex behavior have found that reinforcement is most effective when it is presented immediately after the correct response is made. In order to have the greatest effect, the experimenter should say "Right" _____ after the correct response is made.
16. immediately	17. Saying "right" or showing a learner the correct answer after he responds correctly confirms his correct response. The next time the question arises he is more likely to make the correct response again. *Confirmation of a cor- rect response* r_____s the response.
17. reinforces	18. In the classroom students do various types of learning exercises. The teacher usually collects the written exer- cises, takes them home, corrects them, and returns them to the students the next day. Does this procedure use reinforcement efficiently? _____. It (is, is not) im- mediate reinforcement.
18. No is not	19. Twenty words of a spelling list are the *responses.* Teacher X reads a word, the students write their re- sponse, and the teacher writes the correct spelling on the blackboard. Then the next word is read. Teacher Y reads each word, collects the papers, corrects and re- turns them the next day. Teacher Z reads each word, has the student exchange papers, and gives the correct spelling. Rank these teachers on efficient use of rein- forcement: best_____: next _____: last_____

X (immediately) Z (slight delay) Y (long delay)	20. The teacher who provides the correct spelling immediately after each word in the list confirms the correct responses of the students. Any teacher can show in a classroom experiment that immediate confirmation affects learning. C_____ of correct responses is one type of reinforcement.
Confirmation	21. The findings of both laboratory psychology and educational experimentation show that learning is more efficient if r_____ is given _____ after the correct response occurs.
reinforce- ment immediately	22. Immediately after you answer this item, you will be reinforced by obtaining c_____tion of your correct response.
confirmation	23. In the laboratory the experimenter is the judge of the correctness of the learner's response. In this program, you are the judge of your own response. The confirmation of the correct response to each of these "questions" is the presentation of the correct _____ when you turn the page.
23. answer (don't call yourself wrong if you said "response")	

This type of programing represents the Skinner approach. Note that it presents the *stimulus* (or question item), elicits the correct *response* (or correct answer), and then reinforces this behavior by showing the student the correct answer or *feedback* before he moves on to the next *stimulus* (question item).

Branching (Intrinsic Programing)

Norman Crowder, unlike Skinner, does not construct questions in order to elicit a uniform answer. He utilizes errors to build knowledge and skill. This is the major concept in intrinsic programing. In order to implement this approach, Crowder has developed a technique called branching. This moves the student into another series of frames for reteaching, if the student has been unsuccessful in the original set of questions or frames. This is done by testing the student on each unit immediately. If he fails the test question, the preceding unit of information is reviewed. The nature of his error is explained to him, and he is retested. The test questions are multiple choice, and there is a separate set of correction material for each wrong answer that is given in the multiple choice alternatives. If the student passes the test question, he is then told to go on to the next unit of information and the next text question.

The format for the Crowder system in printed form is called the "scrambled text." The pages are not read consecutively. The student is directed to turn to a particular page after he has chosen his answer. If the answer is incorrect, he is directed to turn to another page; if the answer is correct, to still another page. The student must carefully follow directions at the bottom of each page. The following is an example of the Crowder Method.[2]

Mathematicians frequently are accused of speaking a language that is different from that spoken by the rest of the populace. This accusation is not entirely justified. The language of mathematics is simply ordinary speech extended to include rather unfamiliar symbols as well as words. But the sentences used by mathematicians can be analyzed into subjects and predicates, verbs and nouns, just as ordinary speech can. Since it is important for us to understand the structure of the language of mathematics if we are going to learn to speak that language, let's first be sure we understand the structure of ordinary speech.

Below you will find a multiple-choice question. Pick what you believe is

[2] Norman A. Crowder and Grace C. Martin, *Adventures in Algebra*, Doubleday, Garden City, N. Y., 1961, p. 5.

the right answer to the question and turn to the page indicated after the answer you choose. The question is:

In the sentence "All women are poor drivers," which words are the subject and the verb?

    All women is the subject and *are poor drivers* is the verb.   page 5

    All women is the subject and *are* is the verb.   page 7

    Poor drivers is the subject and *are* is the verb.   page 10

5

(from page 1)

YOUR ANSWER: *All women* is the subject and *are poor drivers* is the verb.

We didn't say that the sentence "All women are poor drivers" consists of a subject and verb and nothing else. There are some words in this sentence that are neither subject nor verb, so after you have designated the subject and verb you should have some words left over.

You have divided the sentence into its subject and predicate. *All women* is the subject, because *all women* is what the sentence is about. *Are poor drivers* is the predicate, because this is what the sentence says about *all women*. Now, the verb is contained in the predicate. Here the verb is the word *are*. This verb is what is called a "linking" verb because it functions as a connecting link between the subject and the words that complete the thought of the sentence.

So now you know which words are the subject and the verb. Go back to page 1 and choose the correct answer.

10

(from page 1)

YOUR ANSWER: *Poor drivers* is the subject and *are* is the verb.

The subject of a sentence is that part of it about which something is said. The sentence "All women are poor drivers" is not about poor drivers. A sentence about poor drivers would be one such as "Poor drivers are a traffic hazard," in which *poor drivers* is the subject. But the sentence "All women are poor drivers" is about *all women,* and *all women* is the subject of the sentence.

Now return to page 1 and choose the correct answer.

There is a great deal of controversy in the field of programing as to the relative merits of "linear programing" and "intrinsic programing." Some of the newer programs are incorporating a little of each.

Until recently, few programs had been written; the process is time consuming, and the number of programers is limited. Those programs developed so far differ as to approach and format, and little may be generalized about constructing programs.

Teaching Machines Versus Programed Textbooks

Presently there are machines on the market which cost between $30 and $30,000. They range from simple metal mechanical machines to electronic machines which use microfilm and audio tape. The production and design of machines has proceeded at a much more rapid pace than has the development of carefully planned and tested programs.

The important thing for the programer to remember is that machines should be built to fit variation in the program. Most of the machines now being marketed will accommodate only one type of program, which greatly limits the machines' instructional potential. For example, if a machine is built to accommodate only multiple-choice items, a programer is limited to writing only such items; whereas, in order to produce a good program, he might wish to include write-in items as well as multiple-choice items. No machine has been built to accommodate every type and variation of program.

Machines, however, have the advantage of being "cheat-proof," since the correct answer to a question is exposed only after the student has given his response. Apparently this feature is not too important because present research shows that the use of machines produces no better results than a series of questions and explanations in the form of a "programed textbook." Booklets and textbooks have the advantage of being portable. They may be carried to the library, to the classroom, or home. This cannot be done with a machine. A student can work from a textbook whenever he has free time; but he can use a machine only when it is available. Teachers may assign materials in programed textbooks as homework. In this way, students prepare away from class without pre-empting class time. This procedure makes it possible to spend class time discussing other facets of the subject matter.

Programing Versus Conventional Methods

Good reading practices have always included elements of programing. For example, most of the better reading series used in the schools start in the first grade with small steps and a controlled vocabulary, proceeding gradually to larger steps and more difficult reading selections. Careful sequencing is inherent in a good basal reading series.

Moreover, much of the reading curriculum is broken into small units similar to the method used in programing. Elementary reading textbooks have short stories, poems, and sometimes, just a few sentences in which students apply their recently learned skills. Reading laboratories, such as the S. R. A. multi-level materials, present short units of work with immediate opportunity for application and reinforcement. Thus the concept of breaking down material into small units is not unique to programing.

Reading teachers have long known the value of rewarding students when they are right. One of the advantages of small reading groups, which allows a teacher to individualize instruction, is that there is more opportunity for the teacher to encourage the student each time he is right. Perhaps that is one of the reasons why children with serious reading disabilities usually have more successful learning experiences in small reading groups rather than in regular classrooms.

We may then ask the question: if so much of programing is already part of good reading instruction, what are the essential differences between programing and the conventional methods of teaching reading?

How does the programed textbook differ from a workbook?

A workbook usually does not teach; it contains practice exercises for drill. If the pupil hasn't learned from the teacher's presentation of the lesson or from the textbook, the workbook serves no purpose. Since a workbook depends upon the teacher to correct the answers, an incorrect response repeated many times may become the behavior pattern. The pupil who makes a correct response may have to wait days or even weeks to learn that he is right. By then the feedback may come too late to reinforce the correct answer because, as psychologists have found, only when a student's correct answer is confirmed immediately will he be likely to give the correct answer again the next time the question is asked.

How does the programed textbook differ from a textbook?

A student reading a textbook may or may not become involved with its content. The information is presented on the page and it is assumed by the author that the student understands what he is reading; rarely does the author require a response from the reader. A program, on the other hand, does require a response from the learner.

A textbook does not reinforce learning at each step. It presents a concept, gives examples, and asks questions at the end of the chapter (which in a sense is a testing rather than a teaching procedure). In programed instruction, the student is involved in every step of the procedure. He must respond to each frame and check his response (reinforcement) before moving on to the next frame.

A textbook teaches by way of broad concepts as seen by the author (with limited trials with students), and assumes that the student understands these concepts. By contrast, the programer in developing a program actually involves the student in the writing of the text by giving him each set of frames to read and respond to, and so learns from the student the number and order of steps he requires to fully understand the concept. The programer, on the basis of the student's responses, revises the program.

How does the programed textbook differ from a classroom lesson?

A programed textbook allows each child to learn at his own rate and select that material which he views as meaningful to him at a particular stage in his development. The teacher cannot pace teaching to meet all the individual differences in learning; nor can she translate facts, concepts, and ideas into the thought forms of pupils at each pupil's stage of intellectual development. One teacher simply cannot individualize all instruction in a classroom of thirty children.

Children differ in their learning skills; in one area they may move rapidly and be leaders and in others they may need more time and attention or, indeed, corrective helps. Even if teachers could know all of the subtle differences among pupils, they would still find it impossible always to make provision for even the most obvious differences. In a reading-skills lesson, half the class might grasp a particular concept long before the teacher has finished with the lesson, whereas the other half might need more explanation, smaller steps, and more time to think and to absorb what is being taught. A teacher must move along in a lesson. If he waits for the slowest pupils, he runs the risk of losing the attention and interest of the rest of the class. (Many a student has developed a learning disability because of the relentless demands of a teacher's "weekly plan.") On the other hand, the child who reads a passage quickly becomes impatient when required to wait for the rest of his classmates. Independent reading by programed textbooks allows each student to move at his own rate; to proceed as rapidly as he can give correct responses; to stop at certain points to reflect upon what he has read.

A classroom lesson offers little opportunity to correct mistakes immediately, since the teacher is often unaware that an individual child has not understood a point or has misinterpreted facts. The student may be learning an incorrect concept or skill and the teacher may not be aware of it for a period of time. In programing, the alert teacher will know exactly when and where an error is made by examining the text which is a written record of how each student responds to a given set of concepts.

How does the programed textbook differ from a film or telecast?

A film or telecast has the same limitations as a textbook with respect to checking concept understandings. The projector or television set moves along at a certain pace, carrying some pupils with it and losing others along the way. The programed textbook, on the other hand, is controlled by the learner; he does his own pacing, stopping when difficulties arise and moving along rapidly when he understands each item. The passive participation in a film or telecast is hard to analyze, as one is never sure whether it is the content or the medium which holds the child's attention.

How does the programed textbook differ from a test?

A test asks a question to which the student gives the answer; it does not teach. When a child answers a question on a test incorrectly, he learns only that he has been wrong. Sometimes test papers are not returned, and a student is never made aware of the fact that he has made a mistake. He, therefore, continues to make the same mistake until it is detected by some other means. Programing, on the other hand, gives the learner immediate information as to the correctness of a response.

Another important difference is that test items are designed to differentiate or measure. In programing, the object is to construct all items so that the student is taught by answering each item correctly (linear programing). Each item or question tests his learning; each correct answer reinforces his learning; teaching and testing are interwoven.

Other Uses of Programing

In a regular classroom, a student who is absent often loses the work he has missed because he cannot recapture what has taken place in the classroom. On the other hand, if he has the program at home with him while he is absent, he at least shares with the rest of the class the basic experience provided in the programed text, even though he does not have the advantage of the classroom discussion.

Since programed instruction is self-instructional, it has vast possibilities for homebound students. The homebound student may become his own instructor with periodic lessons and cumulative evaluation by visiting teachers.

In some schools students work at home with the programed materials. School hours are then devoted to discussion and further exploration of the subject matter presented in the program.

On the college level whole courses are being programed,[3] thus allowing the instructor to deal with more difficult subject matter during the class time. If routine learnings can be programed and studied apart from school hours, entire curricula may soon be changed.

There are no perfect programs and probably there never will be; neither are there perfect classroom lessons or textbooks. However, programing has certain advantages over other methods of teaching. Holland and Skinner [4] list seven advantages:

1. Each student advances at his own rate, the fast learner moving ahead rapidly while the slower learner moves at a speed convenient for him.
2. The student moves on to advanced materials only after he has thoroughly mastered earlier stages.
3. Because of this gradual progression and with the help of certain techniques of hinting and prompting, the student is almost always right.
4. The student is continuously active and receives immediate confirmation of his success.
5. Items are so constructed that the student must comprehend the critical point in order to supply the answer.
6. "Concept" is represented in the program by many examples and syntactical arrangements, in an effort to maximize generalization to other situations.
7. A record of students' responses furnishes the programer with valuable information for future revisions.

However, it would be wise to keep in mind that, although the advantages as listed by Holland and Skinner can point toward effective learning, teaching methods can be appraised only on a basis of the quantity and quality of what is learned. Up to this point, it is too early to make any prediction.

Programing Reading

When we consider the application of programed instruction to the field of reading, there are many questions we may well ask. Can

[3] James G. Holland and B. F. Skinner, *The Analysis of Behavior*, McGraw-Hill, New York, 1961.
[4] *Ibid.*, pp. v–vi.

programed materials be developed in reading? Some feel that certain subjects lend themselves more easily to programing than others. Mathematics, for instance, is clearly defined with a sequence that is inherent in the subject matter. Critical reading, on the other hand, calls for a variety of responses with little room for common or exact responses. However, there are those who feel that critical reading can be programed by providing the learner with criteria rather than facts. If it is assumed that reading can be programed at all, it is then important to decide what skills could be encompassed in such a program. Will children be able to apply the skills they have learned through this method to their reading and study habits? How will we, as teachers, know that children are learning from this method? What will a program in reading look like? Are there any programs in reading now available?

In the area of reading, the following programs are being prepared at the Center for Programed Instruction, a non-profit educational organization supported by grants from the Carnegie Corporation and the Fund for the Advancement of Education.

Critical Reading. Selected passages and topics are being programed to teach students some of the many skills needed for critical reading. The program, consisting of reading passages that include propaganda, advertising materials, other prose, and poetry, is devised to develop a critical understanding of what is written by examining how passages are constructed and the purposes for which they are written.

Developmental Reading. Three reading specialists from the New York Public School system, Junior High School Division, have been assigned to work with the Center to develop a program in reading to include basic reading skills required to do school work. The following experimental units have already been developed: *Contextual Clues; Phonetic Analysis* ("Introduction to Phonetic Analysis," "Initial Consonants," "Final Consonants," "Consonant Blends with Audio Directions," "Consonant 'c'—Hard and Soft Sound," "Consonant 'g'— Hard and Soft Sound"); *Structural Analysis* ("Introduction to Structural Analysis," "Inflected Endings," "Comparisons," "Apostrophe 's,' and "Compound Words"); and *Comprehension Skills* ("Understanding Sentences" and "Main Idea in a Paragraph").

Vocabulary Building. This program in word analysis teaches common Latin and Greek roots and prefixes. The student practices analyzing complicated words as he learns the component parts.

The programs mentioned above are presently being developed through intensive experimentation. None of the programs is as yet completed. The development of such programs is a slow analytical process, but one which throws new light on the learning process and the relative merits of varying approaches.

A programer needs extensive training and practice in the philosophy and techniques of programing before he can be considered skilled. One cannot become a programer from reading these few pages. Programed instruction crystallizes what a good teacher should be able to do in the classroom as part of good teaching procedure. It calls for the highest order of planning.

Until recently, most programing was done by experimental psychologists, but their programs often lacked content suitable for classroom use. Therefore, efforts are now being made to teach programing to experienced teachers—teachers who can communicate with children and who know language levels and the curricula.

Perhaps an even better approach might be that of a team composed of the psychologist to help with cuing and reinforcement techniques and the teacher who would be responsible for the content and the sequence of the frames.

Learning to program can be a valuable experience for any teacher. It is through the experience of constructing frames for programed instruction that the teacher becomes aware of the very thought processes by which a student learns a concept. In programing, one must place each step in proper sequence in order to elicit the desired learner response. The technique of careful sequencing is a discipline which every teacher should have, for it is one of the more creative aspects of planning. When a faulty frame is constructed (one that produces undesirable or incorrect response), the teacher must re-examine the question and reword it to include the proper cues so that the correct response is more probable. The frames which elicit wrong answers from any significant portion of students are by definition poorly constructed frames. If a teacher were to examine every learning experience by first identifying the objective (terminal behavior) and then proceed to plan each step by breaking it down to its stimulus-response elements and then to include steps to insure the use of the information (application), he would be analyzing the task rather than "presenting a lesson."

In programing both the inductive and deductive sequences are effective. Both can be used within the same program. In inductive sequences the principle is the response; in deductive programing the principle is the cue-stimulus. Both these approaches are meaningful to the learner since the principle is reinforced by both a response and a cue-stimulus.

Steps in Programing

The following is a progression of steps through which most programers proceed in order to write a program.

Step I. What is the nature of the group for whom the program is being prepared? Determine the reading ability of the students, their interests, and their backgrounds.

Step II. State your behavioral objectives. What is the terminal behavior that you expect from the student? Example: By adding the ending *er* to a root word to compare two things, you are adding the meaning *more* to the root word.

Step III. Begin drafting frames.

A. Items are usually written on cards. The statement and questions are given on one side of the card and the answer on the reverse side. This provides an immediate reinforcement for each response. The purpose of using cards while developing the program is to facilitate the addition and deletion of items and the modification of the sequence.

Front of Card		*Back of Card*
Stimulus:	When you take away the ending *est* from highest,	Reinforcement: High
Response:	the root word _____ is left.	

B. Include the following techniques in writing the frames:
1. A gradual progression from simple to complex in successive steps ending in a generalization. In Exhibit II, three generalizations are reached in successive steps.
2. A gradual withdrawal of stimulus supports (cues) in successive steps while leading to the generalization (see Exhibit III).

C. Selecting appropriate type of items
1. *Lead-in items* orient the student to a problem and prepare him for *new* information. They do not require a review of old skills

Exhibit II

Successive Steps Leading to Generalization

	1. We can make the word *tall* grow by adding the ending *er*. taller We can make the word *tall* gr_____.

1. grow	2. Words that can grow are called root words.
	    The word tall can grow
	    Tall is a r_____

2. root	3. Add the ending *er* to the root word *tall*. tall_____
3. taller	4. When we take away the ending *er* from the word taller, the root word _____ is left.

all

5. A. _____
   B. _____
   These lines are not the same size.
   One line is *longer* than the other line.
   Line B is the l_____ line.

onger

6. A. _____
   B. _____
   One of these lines is short*er* than the other line.
   Line A is the sh_____ line.

shorter

7. A. _____
   B. _____
   We can *compare* these *two* lines by saying:
   Line B is long__ than line A.

onger

8. A. _____
   B. _____
   You might *compare* the *two* lines this way:
   Line A is short__ than line B.

shorter

9. The sentence *compares two* lines.
   We use the ending *er* to _____ _____ things.
   (Generalization.)

9. compare

two

---

10. Some stars look bright__ than others. The ending *er* used to _____ _____ groups of stars.

---

10. brighter

compare two

---

11. We see *more* light from some stars.

These stars look bright__.

---

11. brighter

---

12. We say that some stars look bright*er* because we s

m___ light from these stars.

---

12. more

---

13. bright   brighter

The ending *er* on the root word *bright* makes tl word mean *more* br____.

---

13. bright

---

14. bright   brighter

Anything that is *more* bright than something else bright__.

brighter

15. Some stars are *nearer* to the earth than others. The
    stars that are *nearer* are m___ *near* the earth.

more

16. near   nearer
    The ending *er* on the word *near* makes that word mean
    m___ near.

more

17. near   nearer
    The ending _____ adds the meaning _____ to the
    root word.
         (Generalization.)

er
more

18. A root word has meaning.
    Many endings also have m_____.

meanings

19. We often add *meaning* to the *meaning* of a root word
    when we add e_____s.
         (Generalization.)

19. endings

Exhibit III

Gradual Withdrawal of Stimuli

1. Which word fits in the sentence?

   The lion gave a loud (*rear, roar*).

---

1. roar

2. Did it help you to look carefully at the word itself when you looked for the word that fits in the sentence? The lion gave a loud roar. (*Yes, No*)

---

2. Yes

3. The lion gave a loud roar.

   Did another word in the sentence help you to know that the right word was "roar"? (*Yes, No*)

126

es

4. The lion gave a loud roar.

   What *word* in the sentence helped you to know that the right word was "roar"?

ion

5. The lion gave a loud roar.

   Did you find the *clue* word "lion" *before* or *after* the word "roar" in the sentence?

efore

6. Can you get help (*a*) from another word in the sentence, and (*b*) from the word itself? (*Yes, No*)

es

7. Now you see that you can use more than one clue at a time to help you find the right word. In the sentence, "The lion gave a loud roar," you looked at: (*a*) what came _____ the word in the sentence, (*b*) at the _____ itself.

efore

ord

nor do they require new information. The following are two examples of lead-in items:

    a. Plants *grow* from their roots. Words can also _____ from their roots (preparation for a set of frames on root words and endings).

    b. The letters of the alphabet have names and *sounds*. The letters of the alphabet have names and _____ (preparation for frames on phonic elements).

2. *Augmenting items* supply new information but do not require the student to make a relevant response to the new information. You are pointing out something that they know and you will be using their information to teach a new skill. Examples (audio):

    a. Listen to the beginning sound in each word:

    STOP   The beginning sound in each _____ is the same.
    STAR   (The students are being prepared to study the
    STICK   initial consonant blends.)

    b. The *main idea* in a sentence tells us the most *important* part of the _____. (The students know how to find the main idea of the sentence and you are now preparing to teach the main idea of a paragraph.)

3. *Review items* require rehearsal of the skill where a problem is restated and a new aspect of the same skill may be introduced. Examples:

Review:
We add the ending *er* to a root word to _____ _____ things.
New Knowledge:
The ending *er* also adds the meaning *more* to the root w_____.

4. *Delayed review items* differ from other items only in the time of presentation. They may be spaced throughout the program and may combine more than one learning step. Example:

When we come to a word we do not know, we can get help from:

    a. Looking at a picture.
    b. The b_____ of a word.
    c. What comes before the word in the sentence.
    d. What comes a_____ the word in the sentence.

5. *Fading items* (those in which the clues are gradually with-

drawn) require the student to gradually fill in the response independent of cues. Example:

    a. Looking at the beginning of the *word* gives you help with the word.

    b. Looking at the beginn__ of the word gives you help with the word.

    c. Looking at the b___g of the word gives you help with the word.

    d. Looking at the _____ of the word gives you help with the word.

6. *Specifying items* presents an established rule or principle. Example:

    The letters a, e, i, o, and u belong to the v____ family.

7. *Dovetailing items* require the student to make separate responses to separate stimuli that correlate with each other. Example:

    A, e, i, o, u are _____. All the other letters of the alphabet are
_____.

8. *Subject matter items* should be classified with respect to a subject matter content. In the reading program straight content frames are not desirable.

Step IV. Edit the Frames.

A. Another programer should check the sequence and construction of the frames.

B. A psychologist should check the cuing and fading techniques.

C. A reading consultant should check vocabulary and thought concepts.

D. A language specialist should check the structural patterns.

Step V. Try the Frames on Students. Program frames should first be tried out with two or three students. If errors are made, ask yourself the following questions:

A. Are the steps too large? If so, additional frames may have to be added in order to lead the student more gradually to the correct response.

B. Is there only one possible answer? If not, rewrite so that only one response is clearly appropriate.

C. Should the sequence be rearranged? If the students consistently respond incorrectly, perhaps the sequence is faulty.

D. Is the vocabulary too difficult? This is usually apparent when the answer does not relate to the question.

E. Are you assuming previous learning that may not exist? A student may need a program on a more elementary and preparatory level.

After a few students have gone through the program, make an item analysis of each student's errors. This should be repeated after every trial.

Step VI. Revise the program. In the light of the item analysis and of the comments of the students, revise your program. Use the new program with a larger group of students. Repeat the tryout and revision procedure until you are satisfied that the students make a minimum of errors. Final refinement should be on a sizable population before publication.

The reader will note that program development calls for constant revision. Constructing programs, like planning good lessons, requires great patience and thorough knowledge of subject matter, and it is very time consuming. Some programers were asked recently to estimate the amount of time necessary to build a program. There was fair agreement that, on the average, a programer could finish a twenty-frame program in ten hours; this figure is for finished items which have been revised and are ready for publication. It is an exacting task but it affords the teacher an opportunity to make a new and detailed analysis of familiar material.

Programing and the Curriculum

Programed instruction as a method of teaching can be applied to many areas of the curriculum. We cannot assume, however, that it is applicable to all curriculum areas. We must decide *how* and *when* programs can best be used. With programed materials, perhaps even to a greater degree than with textbooks, there is a danger that the programer will dictate the curricula.

Skinner says that, given the time to study how an individual learns, one can teach him anything. Programs must be developed to meet the specific and varied requirements of individual students and of the curricula, for, if all children are given the same programed materials, we are defeating one of the primary tenets of programed instruction: individualization of instruction. This would mean that, for a given subject area, many different kinds of programs should be developed.

For example, in reading some children will learn through an emphasis upon structural analysis of words while others will need programs which stress contextual clues. Programs should be built for both types of students.

Programs providing different approaches to a single skill are also needed. Although most students may learn through a conventional approach, some will certainly need unique approaches; for example, an emphasis on tactile and auditory approaches.

As pupils move more rapidly with these materials, more of the curriculum will be covered in a shorter period of time, and levels of learning will be removed or redefined. A youngster will be able to move through the curriculum as quickly or as slowly as his ability allows. No longer will teachers say, "You will have to wait until next year to learn that." Next year's program can be tomorrow's program if the student is ready.

Children have capacities beyond our imagination. With adequate intelligence, perhaps they can far exceed the demands made upon them by our present curricula. Bruner says, "We begin with the hypothesis that any subject can be taught effectively in some intellectually honest form to any child at any stage of development. It is a bold hypothesis and an essential one in thinking about the nature of the curriculum. No evidence exists to contradict this; considerable evidence is being amassed that supports it." [5]

Bruner's statement would imply that, if programs are suitably constructed, it will be possible for a student to learn subjects formerly reserved for the more mature student. Programing can affect the entire curriculum and cause a complete overhaul of what we have been teaching.

Programed instruction will probably never be used as the sole method of instruction, but it will inevitably become an important part of a learning system using various media and agents to accomplish curriculum objectives.

Introducing Programed Materials

Just how important will be the role of programed materials in instruction, and more particularly in reading instruction, has yet to be learned. But there can be little question that this fresh approach

[5] Jerome Bruner, *The Process of Education,* Harvard University Press, Boston, 1961, p. 33.

will be used in the future. It is important, therefore, that all concerned know what is at stake and that any misinformation gleaned from newspaper and magazine articles be dispelled. Here are some points that should be emphasized:

1. Although programs do put students "on their own" in learning skills, this does not mean that the teacher is idle. He has other more important things to turn to. One teacher reported: "Since I have been using programed materials, many of my routine teaching tasks have been taken away from me, and now I have time to talk with small groups of students and discuss problems and explore ideas. The extra time spent working with individuals and small groups has enabled me to help youngsters recognize their own problems."

2. The use of programs can give new insight into the teaching-learning process. Another teacher made this comment: "Because programed instruction enables students to learn so much more quickly, it has made me move faster, and I find that I am going into the course of study of the next grade."

3. There is little question that good programs give students new ways of knowing something and, as such, they add to depth of understanding. As a teacher reports: "Not only do some students have more time for discussion because of going at a faster pace than the rest of the class, but the quality of their discussion seems to be deeper and shows fuller understanding of the subject. Very often they will discuss the program itself and make suggestions for improvements, or they will sometimes take issue with some of the statements."

4. Programed materials help immeasurably with the problem of teaching classes with wide ranges of abilities. One teacher noted how programs helped with slow learners: "Because of this type of instruction, I can identify students who take long periods of time to learn . . . when the class is not working in programed texts, I now make allowances for the slower learners. I find programed material helpful in grouping for instruction. While one group is working with the programed text, I am doing other things with the rest of the class. Unlike so many other grouping situations, this one permits all pupils to have a learning experience even though I give my attention to only one.part of the class."

Teachers must be involved in new approaches to instruction so that they understand and, hopefully, accept their changing role with confidence. Throughout the country, local universities give workshops in the techniques of programing. A school or school system can begin efforts in programing by sending a group of staff members to attend one of these workshops. This group would, in turn, be responsible for conducting a similar workshop when they returned to the school system.

Evaluating Programed Materials

In the next few years the market will be flooded with programs. These programs will doubtless range from very poor to excellent. It will be the responsibility of the school principal, the reading consultant, and the classroom teacher to review these programs and determine which, if any, should be purchased. Then, too, programs developed within the school system should also be subjected to careful appraisal.

Perhaps the greatest training for evaluating programs is the experience of programing. Even a little actual programing experience can help the program evaluator to know what to look for. The following questions suggest criteria for evaluating programed materials:

1. Is the subject matter in the program correct and adequately covered? The teacher and the curriculum expert are the best judges of this. Inaccuracies or omissions in context would invalidate the results.
2. Has sufficient research on the program been conducted?
   a. On what pupil population has the program been developed?
   b. What is the intellectual, socio-economic, and ethnic complexion of the text population?
   c. How many revisions have been made before the final printing?
   d. Has the publisher published a summary of the results of pretests indicating the extent of revisions?
   e. How many students were involved in the experimentation?
3. What is the error rate?
   a. Are the number of errors during the experimental stages fewer then 5 per cent? Low-error rate is but one criterion of program quality. Low-error rates can be obtained with very simple items. If the item can be easily answered without the student learning what the item is supposed to teach, then the program does not control behavior.
4. What does the program propose to teach? What are the objectives of the program?
5. Does the subject matter meet your curriculum requirements?

  a. Does the program meet present course requirements?

  b. Does the program provide for enriching the curriculum content?

 6. Are the items or frames in logical sequence?

  a. Does the program start with a simple concept and build toward a generalization?

  b. Does it include a review of earlier frames?

  c. Are the frames constructed so there are natural stopping places?

 7. Does the program provide for frame format variation?

  a. Does the information presented vary in length from frame to frame?

  b. Do frames vary in the pattern of development? For example, if frames 1, 5, 9, and 13 employ "copying clues" and frames 2, 6, 10, and 14 "initial letter clues," a student quickly learns the pattern which impairs the value of the program.

  c. Are the pictures on the frames interesting and appropriate?

  d. Does the program provide for humor where possible?

  e. If there is an audio portion of the program, is it clear in tone and properly synchronized with the written material?

  f. Is there a variety of vocabulary when the steps are very small and the same thought must be repeated in a number of frames?

 8. Does the program make use of the effective techniques of programing?

  a. Is there sufficient cuing—are the clues clear but not overdone?

  b. Is there a limit to the number of possible responses to a frame?

  c. Does the program move to a final uncued "terminal response"? Can the student make his own synthesis of the information in the program through which he has proceeded?

 9. How is the program written?

  a. Is the vocabulary appropriate to the interest and achievement of the students?

  b. Are the sentences well constructed in a clear and concise manner?

  c. Is there a minimum of idiomatic usage, wordiness, ambiguity?

 10. What is the total length of the program?

  a. Is the program divided into sections? Can a pupil stop after a period of time and pick up the program with interest?

  b. How long is the average work period of a learning session?

After a program has been carefully examined by the faculty, applying the criteria suggested above, the program should then be given to a group of students—a sample that represents the ability and interest levels of the students who will eventually use the programed materials. This experimental group should be observed to note the following:

1. Do they seem interested in the content?
2. Can they proceed without help?
3. How long is there an effective attention span?
4. How many errors were made by each student?
5. What was the quality of the students' discussions after they completed a section of frames?
6. What was their performance on a test constructed by the programer and given after the program was completed?
7. What was their performance on a standardized test?

If the program meets with the approval of all who will be using it and students have had a successful learning experience, then it should be recommended for purchase in quantity.

The Future of Programing

There are many unanswered questions about programing. Teachers know that more than instant reinforcement is necessary to successful learning; constant reinforcement is equally important. Does programing provide this so as to induce long range retention of information? How can we be sure that what is learned is transferred to the functional reading of the student? These are questions that should be asked of any instructional approach, not alone of programing. Too often, new methods are introduced without evaluating their effectiveness in learning. Do intelligent students, capable of grasping larger concepts, resent the confining effect of programing's simple mechanical tracks. Programers try to make provisions for these students by branching (as described on pages 112–113). How satisfactory this technique is, though, we do not know. Does programed instruction, because it shapes terminal behavior, reduce imagination and creativity in students? This question, above all others, should be explored before wholesale introduction of programs throughout the curriculum.

Two thousand years ago, Quintillian asked that the individual student not be neglected and that he be questioned and encouraged to strive for victory (so arranged that he gains it); in this way drawing forth his powers through praise and reward.

Through the years we have used a variety of methods for individualization of instruction. Today, programed instruction represents one of the most exciting new approaches toward this end. It holds promise of fulfilling our hope to involve every student at every step of his learning process to teach him as an individual student. Whether or not this is possible will be determined by careful research and sober evaluation.

Suggested Reading

A Guide to Programed Instruction Materials, Center for Programed Instruction, Department of Health, Education, and Welfare, Government Printing Office, Washington, D. C., 1962.

Eigen, L. D., *The Construction of Frames of an Automated Teaching Program*, Collegiate School Automated Teaching Project, New York, November 1959.

Fry, E. B., G. L. Bryan, and J. W. Rigney, *Teaching Machines: An Annotated Bibliography*, University of Southern California, Los Angeles, Electronics Pers. Res. Group, November 1959.

Galanter, E. H. (Ed.), *Automated Teaching: The State of the Art*, Wiley, New York, 1959.

Lumsdaine, A. A., and R. Glaser, *Teaching Machines and Programed Learning*, National Education Association, Washington, D. C., 1960.

Skinner, B. F., *Verbal Behavior*, Appleton-Century-Crofts, New York, 1957.

————, "The Science of Learning and the Art of Teaching," *Harvard Educational Review*, 1954, 24, pp. 86–97.

————, *Science and Human Behavior*, Macmillan, New York, 1953.

Stolurow, Lawrence, *Teaching by Machine—Cooperative Research*, Department of Health, Education and Welfare, Government Printing Office, Washington, D. C., 1961.

5 Community Resources

In addition to programs initiated and supported by school systems, there are important contributions which community groups can make to reading programs. Local residents skilled in the crafts and professions may be invited to share their talents with school children. If the program is well organized and if the demands on the time of resource personnel prudent, integrated community-school programs can be very effective.

A community program, like a school program, should be fitted to the problems, needs, and resources of the students. In order to do this, members of the professional staff and members of the community should together plan the activity. After the type of activity is decided upon, certain procedures for organization should be set. Some of the points to take into consideration are:

I. Setting criteria for selecting students to participate in the program (such as: students should be talented in or especially interested in the subject; students should be capable of organizing and executing special projects suggested by the activity).
II. Designation of faculty adviser(s) and his responsibilities.
III. Provision of instructional aids (such as study guides).
   A. Study Guides
      1. Topic
         a. Why topic was selected
         b. Sources for preliminary reading
         c. Pivotal points expected to be covered in the lecture
      2. Speaker
         a. General information on background
         b. Specific qualifications for this assignment

3. Suggestions for preparatory group discussion (faculty adviser and participating students): Students should note specific points of information which they wish to gain from lecture session. These will serve as a guide to observation and as a basis for queries during the question period.

B. Lecture Guides (Planned to provide a preliminary overview and to minimize the necessity for note taking during the session. Issued to students and to lecturer as well.)

   1. General outline of session activities.

   2. Accurate listing of specific materials used

      a. Books referred to

      b. Pictures shown

      c. Music played, etc.

   3. Recommended materials for further reading and research.

   4. Suggestions for projects as an outgrowth of the session.

   5. Section for notes.

IV. Suggestions for School Follow-Up

A. Pupils reporting—possible methods:

   1. One resource pupil to each class

   2. All resource pupils in panel report

      a. To individual classes

      b. To assembly

   3. Articles for school newspaper or magazine

B. Teacher reporting—possible methods: each teacher reports

   1. To staff conferences

   2. To departmental conferences

C. Pupil projects (possible contributions to science and arts fair).

There are some extensive community programs currently in operation. Some of the plans described in this chapter are used in varying forms by communities other than those mentioned.

The Intellectual Resource Pool Used Outside School

In South Orange, New Jersey, School District a unique educational experiment was initiated under a grant from the New World Foundation. This experiment invites scientists, social scientists, writers, artists, and other creative citizens in the community to give a new dimension to the public school curriculum. The project is a cooperative venture of the local board of education, the administrative staff of the school system, the PTA Council, and a newly created committee called the Intellectual Resources Pool. Selected students from grades five to twelve attend Saturday morning seminars in various subject areas. These are conducted by experts in the various fields. The seminars are limited to fifteen students selected, according to the teacher's observation, for their creative ability, or their potential ability which might be challenged by his experience. The resource pool is not intended as a substitute for systematic teaching of the body of factual knowledge presented by the classroom teacher. It is an experience which extends the students' knowledge, allowing them an opportunity to discover new things about the world from practicing research scientists, writers, artists, and social scientists. The following is a description of the plans for two seminars conducted in South Orange for students with fifth and sixth grade reading ability.

Seminar 1—Analyzing newspaper articles

The seminar leader is Mr. Eliot Tozer, a press representative of the Columbia Broadcasting System television network and a free lance writer. The group will begin by discussing, as case histories, articles by Mr. Tozer that have appeared in such national magazines as *Popular Science, Boy's Life,* and *Atlantic Monthly,* along with news stories and press releases that he has written. A concrete approach to writing will be established by Mr. Tozer who will comment on how a writer gathers material, writes, submits, and rewrites pieces for newspapers and magazines. At the same time, the group will analyze the newspaperman's job and dissect current articles, noting, for example, plays in which prejudice is the central theme, the use of "color" words, the incidence of half-truths, as well as newswriting that is objective and, even if interpretive, honest. Given these realistic insights into the world of popular writing, students should grow up into discriminating newspaper readers and, at least in some cases, capable newspaper writers.

Seminar 2—Analyzing poems

The seminar leader, Mr. Robert Sennish, is an instructor in literature at Brooklyn College, New York. The group will first read, analyze, evaluate poems; then it will write poems. The reading will be systematic, and students will analyze, step-by-step, the sense of a poem, its rhyme, meter, and imagery before arriving at a critical understanding of what the poem "means." Discussions will aim to show the student that reading for meaning and reading for pleasure usually amount to the same thing. Because the reading will be intensive, it is quite possible that only one or two poems will be read during the entire seminar. Given this formal background in which both the discipline and the vitality of poetry are emphasized, the student will then be urged to transform what he has privately observed and felt into that public thing we call a poem.

Similar plans can be applied to other phases of reading. Novelists, essayists, poets, playwrights, and journalists living in a community may be invited to participate in extracurricular seminars. Selected students would benefit from this experience. No book, film, or classroom lesson can approximate a "live" lecture by the artist himself. However, such a plan should be well organized in order to gain optimum benefit from this type of supplementary activity.

The Intellectual Resource Pool Used in School

Another extension of a community resource plan is to invite authors into the school system to lecture during the regular classroom period. Usually several classes are grouped together for such lectures. If the guest is able to give additional time he may circulate among the students and meet them for small group discussions. The discussions may take the form of students and author exchanging ideas about the writings of both the author and the student.

Community intellectual resources may be extended to include workshops and field trips for teachers, conducted by writers, journalists, and other craftsmen. These workshops or field trips may be part of an in-service program. Such programs would bring teachers in personal contact with people who are practitioners in the various fields. Rockland County in New York State currently employs this type of program.

Public Education Groups (School Volunteers)

In New York City, the Public Education Association initiated "The School Volunteer Reading Help Program" which is an experiment in the use of volunteers to supplement the teaching of reading done by the classroom teacher in the elementary and junior high school. The program aims to raise the reading level and improve related language skills of children who have been selected by the teachers and principal for reading help. Such children are classified in two categories:

1. Children with IQ's of at least 85 who are no more than two years

behind in reading, if such retardation is not the result of severe behavioral or emotional problems.

2. Those children who are reading at grade level but whose IQ's indicate that grade level is, in effect, a retardation, since their potential is not being realized. Such children can be helped to develop vocabulary, to understand concrete and abstract ideas relating to their reading, to read for pleasure and intellectual profit, and to gain self-confidence.

The volunteers who are selected to serve in the reading program have good educational backgrounds, are warm, stable adults who can establish a relaxed, objective relationship with children and who have indicated a special interest in this type of service.

The volunteers attend lectures and participate in discussions led by educators who are trained in reading techniques. Basic philosophies of reading, the methods used in teaching reading in the elementary and secondary schools, and techniques which are valuable in dealing with common reading problems are discussed. Each volunteer is encouraged to use her talents and skills to adapt these techniques to meet the special needs of the child with whom she is working. Conferences between the principal, the child's teacher and the volunteer acquaint the volunteer with the background and needs of the child, and keep the teacher informed of the child's reading problems and progress as noted by the volunteer.

In addition to lectures and conferences, workshops are provided on a regular schedule. School reading consultants conduct these workshops for the purposes of preparing new volunteers-in-training for the program and continuing the education of practicing volunteers. Exhibit I is a guide for such a workshop.

The volunteer, in addition to helping with the basic skills (as described in the Workshop Guide), is in a position to stimulate further interest in reading by:

1. Reading to and with the child.
2. Listening as the child reads.
3. Stimulating the child's interest in books.
4. Opening new horizons through discussion.
5. Providing books for the child to read at home.
6. Using experimental and practice material on the basis of information furnished by the teacher.
7. Maintaining a journal for each child which may serve as a source of information for both teacher and volunteer.

Exhibit I

Workshop for P. E. A. Volunteers

I. Establishing relationships with pupils
II. What to expect from pupils
    A. Regularity in attendance.
    B. Notebook.
    C. Fulfillment of assignments.
III. Keeping an anecdotal record of contact with pupils
    A. Date.
    B. Skill taught.
    C. Material covered.
    D. Pupil attitude and response.
    E. Progress noted.
IV. Planning
    A. Become familiar with the material in advance.
    B. Present the aim of the lesson.
    C. Know how you plan to achieve the aim.
    D. Establish vocabulary before narrative material is presented.
    E. Prepare some pivotal questions in advance—both factual and thought provoking—how, why, what do you think, etc.
V. Suggested area of emphasis—comprehension skills in sequence
    A. Finding the main idea of a sentence.
    B. Finding the general significance of a paragraph or the main idea of the paragraph.
    C. Locating the sentence in the paragraph which contains the main idea; leading to the conclusion that it can be found at the beginning, middle, or end of a paragraph.
    D. Proving the relationship of other sentences to the main idea sentence.
    E. Providing a main idea sentence when none is given.
    F. Recognizing extraneous facts.
    G. Drawing inferences from a sentence or a paragraph—new facts based on stated facts.
    H. Reading critically to distinguish between fact and fiction, fact and opinion.
VI. Some sources of material
    A. Pupil texts, workbooks, trade books.
    B. Newspapers and magazines for headlines, cartoons, advertisements, pictures, stories, etc.

Reading is a skill which takes some children longer to acquire than others, and, as with any skill, practice leads to achievement. The friendly interest of a helpful adult will often not only improve the reading skill of these children, but also encourage a feeling of excitement about reading and will inspire them with self-confidence in their ability to master the printed page.

The school volunteer program is now in its third year in New York City and is being extended to reach a number of additional schools. The important ingredient to insure success in this program is constructive planning between the school volunteer group and the professional staff of the school system.

Reading Counseling and Teaching Centers

This type of project which is presently being proposed to the United States Office of Education calls for the establishment of reading counseling and teaching centers on Saturdays for children who have normal ability but are retarded in reading. The purpose of these centers would be to find the causes of extensive retardation, to establish an actual learning situation which will help the child overcome his handicap, and to serve as a training center for new teachers. These reading centers would be housed in either school buildings or community centers and sponsored by schools, universities, civic or foundation funds, or any combination of these resources.

Admission to the Saturday instructional classes would be without charge to the individual child. With the approval of the parent, the school principals would make recommendations for children to be enrolled in the program. Parents must also agree to participate in a program consisting of several private interviews and group conferences regarding their child's reading problems. If the reading centers are housed in community recreational buildings, combining both programs—instructional and recreational—is recommended. Reluctant students might be attracted to the program if they knew that they could swim or play basketball either before or after the instructional phase of the day's activity. Such a center also lends itself to a combination with school or community music programs on Saturdays.

The centers would be staffed with a director, reading consultants, psychologists, social workers, a guidance counselor, secretaries, a graphic arts teacher, and an audio-visual technician. Members of the staff, with the exception of the reading consultant, may be drawn from the community, thus increasing the pool of available services. Teachers from the schools from which the pupil population for the center is drawn, would be selected to act as observing and participating teachers in the center. They should be given either compensation for their services or course credit, if in-service courses are required by the school system. They would observe the reading consultant and the instructional approaches used by him in both small and large groups. They would learn how to discover a child's reading disabilities, note progress and relate this progress to their own school program. In this way the child's corrective and classroom experiences would be integrated.

Such reading centers would also serve the purpose of pre-service teacher-education laboratories. Student teachers might be invited to observe both the instructional and counseling phases of the program. They might also assist in preparing instructional materials.

In the reading counseling and teaching centers, the reading consultants would work with individuals, small groups, and large groups, depending upon the particular needs of the children. Diagnostic tests administered to all students enrolled in the center would indicate reading disabilities. On this basis students would be grouped and individual programs developed. Closed-circuit television might be utilized as a method of working with large groups. Instructional materials such as overhead visual aids, slides, filmstrips, and charts would be developed by the audio-visual technician under the supervision of the reading consultant.

The consultant, together with the guidance personnel, would plan meetings with parents to help them understand the child's reading difficulties and their role in helping the child. Group counseling sessions for parents could take place at the same time that the children are working with the reading consultant. The combined approach of reading specialists, psychologist, social worker, classroom teacher, student teacher, guidance counselor and parent provides the best climate for a successful integrated reading experience for the child.

Educators talk a great deal about involving the community, but rarely do they think of tapping the intellectual resources of the community to enrich the educational experiences of both students and the professional staff as indicated above.

The pooling of resources can create a highly effective program and, more than any other approach, can lead a community to be actively interested in the education of the children.

Suggested Reading

Betts, E. A., "Parents and Teachers Want To Know About Reading," *Education,* 78 (January 1958), pp. 289–299.

California State Department of Education, "The Preparation of Teachers for Homebound Community Relations," *Bulletin of the State Department of Education,* 22, No. 8, 1953.

Hardimann, Ruth, and John T. Robinson, *How To Utilize Favorable, and To Cope With Unfavorable Community Influences in Improving Reading,* Supplementary Educational Monographs, No. 72, pp. 68–77, University of Chicago Press, Chicago, 1950.

Osborne, E. G., *Parent Teacher Partnership,* Bureau of Publications, Teachers College, Columbia University, New York, 1959.

Stout, Irving W., and Grace Langdon, *Parent Teacher Relationships,* What Research Says to the Teacher, No. 16, National Education Association, Washington, D. C., 1958.

What Should Our Schools Accomplish, National Citizens Commission for Public Schools, New York, 1955.